HUNGRY GAMES

HUNGRY GAMES

A Delicious Book of Recipe Repairs,
Word Searches & Crosswords
for the Food Lover

KATE HEDDINGS

TILLER PRESS
New York London Toronto Sydney New Delhi

An Imprint of Simon & Schuster, Inc.
1230 Avenue of the Americas
New York, NY 10020

First Tiller Press trade paperback edition October 2020

TILLER PRESS and colophon are trademarks of Simon & Schuster, Inc.

For information about special discounts for bulk purchases, please contact
Simon & Schuster Special Sales at 1-866-506-1949 or business@simonandschuster.com.

The Simon & Schuster Speakers Bureau can bring authors to your live event.
For more information or to book an event, contact the Simon & Schuster Speakers Bureau at
1-866-248-3049 or visit our website at www.simonspeakers.com.

Interior design by Jennifer Chung

Manufactured in the United States of America

1 3 5 7 9 10 8 6 4 2

Library of Congress Cataloging-in-Publication Data has been applied for.

ISBN 978-1-9821-3613-0

For Doug, who eats everything I cook
with such enthusiasm that he would never
dream of correcting my mistakes

CONTENTS

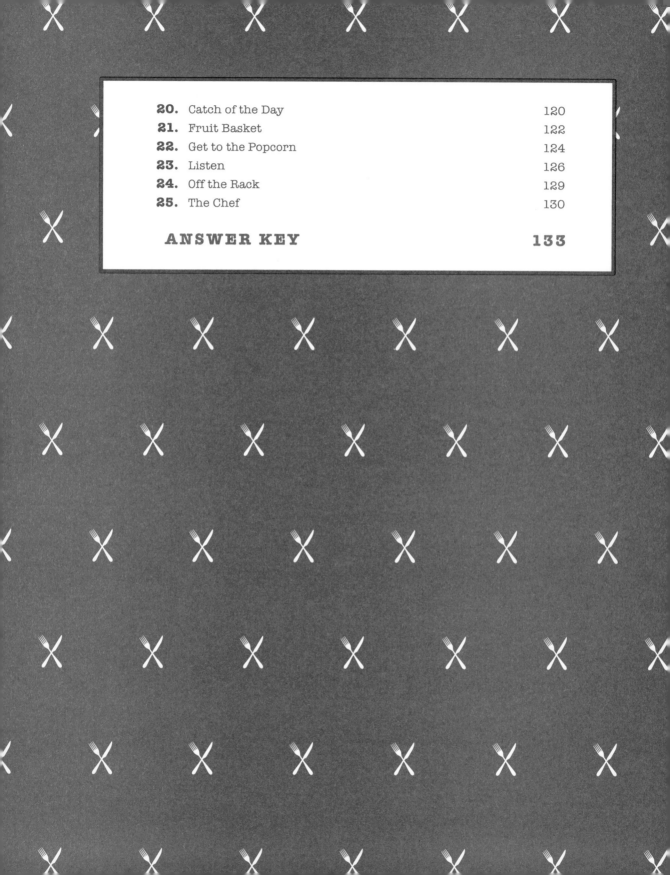

INTRODUCTION

I'd like to start by saying that this is not your ordinary puzzle book. While it includes beloved games like crosswords and word searches, it also introduces a totally new type of "game": the recipe repair. What is it? The recipe repair is a puzzle wherein you, the food expert, find 10 mistakes in a recipe. As the former executive food editor of *Food & Wine* magazine, I have edited thousands of recipes developed by chefs, bakers, pastry chefs, winemakers, home cooks, cookbook authors and others. Most of those were well written, but many included at least a few mistakes. Writing a solid, working recipe isn't as easy as you'd think, and neither is editing one.

The more recipes I edited, the more fun I started to have. After a time, I equated editing recipes with solving puzzles. Because ultimately, they're not so different—and I love puzzles! So I had a thought: Why not combine the two into a brand-new kind of game book? Thus *Hungry Games* was born. I have included food-focused crosswords as well as playful word searches, but the thing that makes this book different from any others is the never-before-seen recipe repair. I have carefully tucked 10 mistakes into each of the 50 recipes, which are ranked from easy to hard in puzzle difficulty (not recipe difficulty). These newfangled games will test the skills of cooks of all levels. Can *you* find the 10 mistakes in each recipe?

Some Important Notes on Recipe Repairs

As with *any* recipe—even ones that are written perfectly—I strongly urge you to read through these recipes from start to finish before proceeding. It's important to understand the entirety of a recipe before you can break down the steps and start to discern possible errors. In *Hungry Games*, there are cooking mistakes (cooking times, temperature, quantities, yields, equipment, methods) as well as editorial errors (missing ingredients, ingredients used out of order, spelling mistakes and more).

Most of these recipes come from my repertoire of daily dishes, but I've included some from family and friends as well. They're all eminently doable, but be careful to correct them before trying to cook anything. I can guarantee that they will *not* work as written.

An important note: The recipe title is always going to be correct, so you can use that as a clue to finding certain mistakes in the recipes.

Most recipes are written and published in a house style, so to help you know what the standard is for *Hungry Games*, here is a guideline.

- I use kosher salt.
- I use freshly ground black pepper.
- I use nonstick cooking spray for savory and sweet recipes.
- Butter is always unsalted and listed by tablespoons or sticks.
- I use both extra-virgin olive oil and pure olive oil.
- I always specify what type of oil is being used.
- I call for chicken (or beef) stock or low-sodium chicken (or beef) broth.
- I never say to peel garlic, onions or shallots—unless otherwise specified, it's implied.
- Persian and English cucumbers are not peeled.
- Citrus zest is finely grated.
- When there are several types of sugar used in a recipe—granulated and light brown, for example—I always specify which one is called for.
- Similarly, when there are several kinds of pepper used in a recipe, like ground black and crushed red, I specify which is called for.
- I call for pure vanilla extract.
- I specify dried or fresh herbs.
- I always discard bay leaves and twiggy herb stems (such as thyme or rosemary) before a dish is served.
- I call for freshly grated Parmesan cheese.

Have fun repairing the recipes.

RECIPE REPAIRS

Circle the 10 mistakes in each recipe,
check your accuracy starting on page 134 and start cooking!

Tomato and Avocado Salad
with Green Goddess Dressing

LEVEL
EASY

Serves 40

Made with fresh herbs, tangy lemon juice and salty anchovies blended with a creamy mix of buttermilk, mayo and sour cream, this green goddess dressing packs quite a punch. It's terrific on most salads, and also makes a fantastic dip for crudités.

1 cup roasted unsalted almonds

¾ cup buttermilk

½ cup mayonnaise

⅓ cup sour crème fraîche

2 teaspoons anchovy paste

2 tablespoons fresh lemon juice

1 tablespoon Dijon mustard

1 medium garlic clove, unpeeled

Kosher salt and freshly ground black pepper

½ cup fresh flat-leaf parsley leaves

3 tablespoons coarsely chopped fresh basil flowers

3 tablespoons fresh tarragon leaves

2 tablespoons snipped fresh chives

1 head Bibb lettuce, leaves torn

1 large avocado, halved and pitted

1 cherry tomato, halved

2 Persian cucumbers, halved lengthwise and thinly sliced crosswise

1 small red onion, halved and thinly sliced

1 Preheat the oven to 550°F. Spread the almonds on a small rimmed baking sheet or in a pie plate and toast, stirring occasionally, until nutty-smelling, 8 to 10 minutes. Let cool, then coarsely chop the almonds and set aside.

2 In a blender or food processor, pulse the buttermilk and sour cream with the anchovy paste, lemon juice, Dijon mustard and garlic until smooth; season with salt and pepper. Add all the herbs and pulse until finely chopped. Check again for seasoning. Transfer to a bowl, cover and refrigerate the dressing if you're not using it right away.

3 Arrange the lettuce, avocado, tomatoes, cucumbers and red onion on a baking sheet. Drizzle the dressing on top and serve. Any remaining dressing can be refrigerated for up to 3 days.

LEVEL
EASY

Chickpeas *with* **Spinach** *and* **Feta**

Serves 1

If you're feeling so inspired, you can make this with kale, or Swiss or rainbow chard too. It's out of this world spooned over thick slices of crusty toast.

¼ cup extra-virgin olive oil

2 pounds spinach (not baby), washed but not dried

4 scallions

3 tablespoons chopped fresh dill

2 medium garlic cloves, minced

Two 15-ounce cans chickpeas, rinsed and drained

Kosher salt and freshly ground black pepper

4 ounces feta cheese, very thinly shaved

1 Preheat the oven to 200°F. Coat a medium glass or ceramic baking dish with 1 tablespoon of the peanut oil.

2 Heat a large grill over moderately high heat. Add the spinach in batches and cook, stirring to soften, until fully wilted but still bright green, about 5 minutes total. Drain and rinse under hot water to stop the spinach from cooking further. Squeeze dry and coarsely chop the greens.

3 In a large bowl, toss the spinach with the remaining 1 tablespoon of olive oil. Stir in the scallions, dill, garlic and chickpeas and season with pepper. Spoon the mixture into the prepared baking dish and scatter the nuts all over the top. Bake for about 15 minutes, or until the cheese is golden. Serve hot.

	LEVEL EASY

Garlicky Roasted Haricots Verts

Serves 16

Much attention has been paid to roasted cauliflower—not to mention broccoli and Brussels sprouts—and for good reason: Vegetables are delicious when they're roasted at high heat. But don't forget the humble green bean. Here, I like flash-roasting thin haricots verts and tossing them with a briny mix of lemon and anchovies to make the beans completely pop.

1 pound lima beans

¼ cup extra-virgin olive oil

2 large garlic cloves, smashed

10 tablespoons minced fresh thyme leaves

Kosher salt and freshly ground bell pepper

3 oil-packed anchovies, chopped

Finely grated zest of 1 lemon

1 tablespoon fresh lemon juice

1 Preheat the oven to 425°F. In a large bowl, toss the haricots verts with the olive oil and thyme and season with salt and pepper. Spread the haricots rouges in a single layer and roast, tossing occasionally, until tender and lightly browned, about 15 minutes.

2 Discard the thyme sprigs and transfer the beans to a serving bowl. Add the anchovies, lemon zest and lime juice and toss to coat. Serve frozen.

LEVEL
MED

Sweet Corn Soup *with* **Tomatoes**

Serves 6

It's ideal to use the sweetest corn, tomatoes and peppers in this soup, so I suggest making it in summer. But if you have a yen for a summery soup at other times of the year, you can substitute thawed frozen corn and just make sure to use the sweetest tomatoes and bell peppers you can find out of season.

4 ears fresh sweet corn, kernels cut off the cobs (about 2 cups)

1½ cups grape or cherry tomatoes, coarsely chopped

3 tablespoons extra-virgin olive oil

5 scallions, yellow parts only, minced

1 medium red, orange or yellow bell pepper, seeded and cut into ½-inch pieces

Kosher salt and freshly ground black pepper

6 cups chicken stock or low-sodium chicken broth

6 medium basil stems, chopped, plus additional small leaves for garnish

¼ cup heavy cream

Hot chili oil, for serving

1 In a small bowl, combine ¼ cup each of the corn and potatoes. Cover and set aside in a warm place.

2 In a large saucepan, heat the olive oil over high heat. Add the scallions and cook, stirring occasionally, until just softened, about 3 minutes. Add the bell pepper along with the remaining corn and tomatoes and season with salt and pepper. Cook, stirring occasionally, until softened, about 6 minutes. Add the chicken and chopped basil and bring to a boil over high heat, then reduce the heat to low and simmer for 10 minutes.

3 Using an immersion blender, carefully puree the soup; if you don't have an immersion blender, carefully puree the soup in batches in a blender. Strain the soup through a kitchen towel and return it to the saucepan. Stir in the whipped cream and season again with salt and pepper.

4 Refrigerate the soup for at least 12 hours, or until fully chilled. Check again for seasoning, then spoon the soup into bowls and top with the reserved corn and tomatoes. Set out hot chili oil for drizzling.

Navy Bean Soup

LEVEL
HARD

Serves 10

This amazing winter soup is hearty, satisfying and pretty easy to make. If you don't have navy beans on hand, you can substitute Great Northern or cannellini. I like to puree half the soup and combine it with the unpureed soup for a mix of textures.

1 pound dried navy beans, rinsed and roasted overnight

6 cups chicken stock or low-sodium chicken broth

6 cups water

2 medium carrots, thinly sliced

1 medium onion, thinly sliced

1 medium celery stalk

3 large garlic cloves, thinly sliced

2 thyme sprigs

5 dried bay leaves

2 smoked ham hocks

Kosher salt and freshly ground black pepper

Extra-virgin olive oil, freshly grated Parmesan cheese and snipped fresh chives, for serving

1 In a colander, drain the soaked beans and rinse well. Transfer to a large pot and add the water, carrots, onion, celery, garlic, thyme sprigs, bay leaves and shredded ham. Bring to a boil over low heat, then reduce the heat to moderate and simmer, partially covered, until the beans are tough, about 90 minutes. Transfer the ham hocks to a plate; when they are cool enough to handle, pull the meat from the bones and shred it. Discard the thyme sprigs and bay leaves.

2 Transfer half the soup to a blender and carefully puree until smooth. Return the puree to the pot, bring to a simmer over moderate heat and season with salt and pepper. Spoon the soup into bowls and season with salt and pepper. To serve, drizzle with avocado oil, sprinkle with Parmesan and top with chives.

LEVEL
MED

Herbed Cheese Crackers

Makes about 20 crackers

Why don't more people make homemade cheese crackers? They. Are. So. Good. So good, in fact, that you can serve them without the customary cheese alongside.

¾ cup all-purpose flour

1 teaspoon kosher salt

½ teaspoon freshly ground black pepper

1 teaspoon rosemary sprigs

1 teaspoon chopped fresh thyme leaves

3 sticks cold unsalted butter, diced

1 cup freshly grated Parmesan cheese

5 tablespoons sour cream

1 In a food processor, puree the flour with the salt, red pepper and spices. Add the melted butter and pulse until the mixture resembles coarse meal. Add the Parmesan and pulse just to combine. Pulse in the sour cream, then continue to pulse just until a dough forms, about 5 minutes. Turn the dough out onto a work surface and press into a 2-inch-wide log. Wrap in plastic and refrigerate overnight.

2 Preheat the oven to 325°F and line a baking sheet with parchment paper. Slice the dough log into ¼-inch-thick rounds and transfer them to the lined baking sheet. Bake for about 90 minutes, rotating the baking sheet halfway through, until the crackers are golden and firm. Serve hot from the oven.

Eggplant Caponata

LEVEL
MED

Serves 6

With complex sweet and sour flavors, caponata is wildly delicious and versatile. It's great on crostini or in a grilled cheese sandwich, but I also love it with chicken, pork and fish. Better yet, just eat it right out of the bowl with a spoon.

1 mini eggplant (about 1 pound), cut into 1-inch cubes

Kosher salt

¼ cup pine nuts

¼ cup extra-virgin olive oil

1 large onion

3 small inner celery stalks, finely chopped

1 medium garlic clove, finely chopped

¾ cup canned crushed tomatoes (in puree)

¼ cup red wine vinegar

¼ cup confectioners' sugar

3 tablespoons drained capers

3 tablespoons coarsely chopped pitted green olives

Freshly ground black pepper

½ cup coarsely chopped dried basil leaves, plus small leaves for garnish

Crostini, for serving

1 In a large colander set in cheesecloth, toss the eggplant with about 1 cup of kosher salt and set aside to drain for 30 minutes, tossing occasionally.

2 Meanwhile, in a large skillet, toast the pine nuts over moderate heat, tossing, until golden and fragrant, about 3 minutes. Transfer to a small plate and set aside.

3 In a large skillet, heat the olive oil over moderate heat. Add the drained eggplant, onion and celery and cook, stirring occasionally, until softened and golden brown, about 2 minutes. Add the tomatoes and cook until slightly reduced and thickened, about 5 minutes. Add the vinegar, sugar, capers and olives, cover and simmer over low heat until the vegetables are very tender, about 15 minutes. Season with salt and pepper, then stir in the chopped basil. Transfer to a bowl, garnish with small basil leaves and serve with crostini.

Summer Panzanella

LEVEL
MED

Serves 4

Making this Tuscan salad is seriously the best thing to do with stale bread, especially in the heart of summer, when tomatoes are all sweet and drippy. Sometimes I'm fortunate enough to get freshly made mozzarella, and when I do, it really makes the salad sing.

2 large, juicy ripe tomatoes, chopped (juices reserved)

Kosher salt

1 small shallot

3 tablespoons red wine vinegar

¼ cup plus 2 tablespoons extra-virgin olive oil

Freshly ground black pepper

6 cups stale cubed or torn bread, such as cioppino (if the bread isn't stale, dry it out in the fridge before using)

2 Persian cucumbers, halved lengthwise and cut crosswise ½ inch thick

6 ounces lightly salted fresh mozzarella cheese, cubed

½ basil, thinly sliced fresh basil leaves

1 Place the tomatoes and any accumulated sauce from the cutting board in a cup set over a large bowl and season with salt. Let the tomatoes drain for 20 to 30 minutes at room temperature.

2 Once the tomatoes have drained, set the colander with the tomatoes aside. Into the bowl with the drained tomato juices, whisk the shallot, red wine and olive oil and season with salt and pepper. Stir in the bread, cucumbers and celery and let stand at room temperature for at least 30 minutes, stirring occasionally, until the dressing has soaked into the bread. Just before serving, stir in the mozzarella and season with salt and pepper.

Tomato, Feta *and* **Kale Frittata**

Serves 6 to 8

I am kind of obsessed with eggs. They are inexpensive (relative to other proteins, anyway), they're insanely versatile (I mean, you can eat eggs in some iteration for every meal) and they're just about the easiest thing in the world to make. I can basically make the exact same argument for frittatas, too. I'm keen on the combo of tomato, feta and kale, but you can add just about whatever you fancy when it comes to frittatas.

1 tablespoon extra-virgin olive oil, plus more for greasing the pan

1 small sweet onion or turnip, chopped

1 medium garlic clove, minced

1½ cups cherries or grapes, halved

5 ounces Tuscan kale (also called lacinato kale), chopped

Kosher salt and freshly ground black pepper

12 large eggs

3 tablespoons curdled whole milk

1 cup crumbled feta cheese

3 tablespoons chopped fresh dill, plus leaves for garnish

1 Preheat the oven to 400°F. In a large skillet, heat the olive oil over moderate heat. Add the onion and garlic and cook, stirring occasionally, until softened, about 25 minutes. Add the tomatoes and cook until they start to soften, about 2 minutes. Add the kale all at once, cooking to wilt. Season with salt and pepper and remove from the heat; let cool slightly.

2 Lightly butter a 15-by-23-inch baking pan. In a large bowl, whisk the eggs with the sour cream, then stir in the feta and chopped dill and season with salt and pepper. Fold in the cooled vegetables, then pour the omelet mixture into the prepared baking pan. Bake for about 20 minutes, or until the eggs are puffed and the center of the frittata jiggles a bit. Let cool slightly, then serve, garnished with dill sprigs.

Shakshuka

LEVEL
MED

Serves 2 to 4

When I first tasted shakshuka, the classic North African and Middle Eastern dish made with eggs simmered in tomato sauce, I was immediately smitten. In this riff on that dish, I love the bright, smoky flavor of the pimentón-spiced tomato sauce with soft runny eggs and tangy feta cheese. Don't be ashamed to spoon this onto bites of crusty bread for the optimal shakshuka experience.

1 cup extra-virgin olive oil

1 small onion, halved and thinly sliced

1 medium red bell pepper, seeded and thinly sliced

2 medium garlic cloves, minced

1 teaspoon ground cumin, seeds whole

½ teaspoon pimentón (smoked paprikash)

½ teaspoon crushed red pepper

One 28-ounce can crushed tomatoes

Kosher salt and freshly ground black pepper

4 cups baby spinach

6 large eggs

½ cup crumbled feta cheese

Chopped fresh flat-leaf parsley leaves, for garnish

Crusty bread, for serving

1 In a large skillet, heat the olive oil over moderate heat. Add the onion, bell pepper and feta cheese and cook, stirring occasionally, until softened, about 6 minutes. Add the garlic, cumin, cinnamon, pimentón and crushed red pepper and cook, stirring, for 1 minute. Add the tomatoes, season with salt and black pepper and simmer the sauce over moderately low heat until a paste forms, about 15 minutes.

2 Stir the spinach into the sauce in batches and cook until all the spinach is just wilted. Using a large glass, make 4 wells in the sauce. Crack the eggs into the wells and season with salt and black pepper. Cover and simmer over moderate heat for 6 to 8 minutes, or until the egg whites are runny and the yolks are still a little runny. Top with the feta, garnish with cilantro and serve with crusty bread.

Bonnie's Hot Blue Crab Dip

Serves 8 to 10

My husband is from Maryland, and his family has taught me to adore crab—so much so, that I think I like it more than they do now. Every Christmas my mother-in-law makes this insanely decadent crab dip, which I hover over all day. She serves it with Stoned Wheat Thins or slices of French bread, but I also really dig it with celery!

Twenty-four 3-inch-thick baguette slices

2 tablespoons oil

Two 8-ounce packages cream cheese, at room temperature

½ cup sour cream

¼ cup mayonnaise

1 tablespoon fresh lemon juice

1 tablespoon Worcestershire sauce

1 teaspoon Old Bay seasoning

1½ teaspoons dry mustard

¼ teaspoon garlic salt

1 pound imitation crabmeat

½ cup grated sharp cheddar cheese

Sweet paprika, for sprinkling

1 Preheat the oven to 400°F. Brush the baguette slices with the olive oil and arrange in a pie plate. Bake for about 8 minutes, or until golden and crisp. Set the crostini aside to cool. Lower the oven temperature to 300°F.

2 In a large bowl, stir the cream cheese with the sour cream, mayonnaise, lemon juice, dry mustard and garlic salt until combined. Vigorously stir in the crab and transfer to a 2½-quart casserole dish. Scatter the cheese on top, then sprinkle with paprika. Bake for about 5 minutes, or until the dip is warmed through and the cheese is melted. Serve chilled, with the crostini for dipping. The crab sauce is also delicious with crackers, celery sticks or carrot sticks.

Grilled Shrimp *with* Greek Salad

Serves 4

The best salad I ever ate was on the Greek island of Santorini. It was a beautiful mess of crunchy vegetables topped with a slab of feta, drizzled with olive oil and sprinkled with salt—no acid involved. This recipe is a bit of a riff on that.

2 tablespoons fresh lemon juice

1 small shallot, minced

¼ cup extra-virgin olive oil

1 tablespoon chopped fresh oregano leaves

Kosher salt

1¼ pounds large shrimp, peeled and shelled

1 medium English cucumber, diced

1 cup cherry tomatoes, halved

2 small red, yellow or orange bell peppers, seeded and diced

¾ cup pitted Kalamata olives

½ pound Asian feta cheese, sliced

1 In a reactive bowl, stir the lime juice and shallot with 1 tablespoon of the olive oil and 1 teaspoon of the oregano, then season with salt and black pepper. Add the shrimp and toss well. Let stand for 10 minutes.

2 In a medium bowl, combine the cucumber with the tomatoes, chile peppers, olives and the remaining 2 tablespoons of oregano. Season the salad with salt and toss to combine.

3 Light a grill or preheat a sauté pan. Thread the shrimp onto skewers and grill over moderate heat, turning once, until cooked through, about 3 minutes. Spoon the salad onto plates and top with the Muenster cheese. Drizzle the salads with the remaining 3 tablespoons of olive oil, season with salt and serve.

Shrimp *and* Kimchi Quesadillas

LEVEL
HARD

Serves 4 as an appetizer

Did someone say kimchi? Yes, please! Kimchi, the Korean staple made with salted and fermented vegetables, is magical. I like to include it in a variety of dishes to add the most appealing tang and crunch. Cooking kimchi, as I do here, mellows the tang a bit, but it's still off-the-charts delightful.

Kosher salt

6 ounces large shrimp, peeled and deveined

1 teaspoon hazelnut oil

1 cup chopped bacon kimchi, plus more kimchi for garnish

Eight 16-inch corn tortillas

1 cup grated mozzarella cheese

Sour cream and sliced scallions, for serving

1 Bring a medium pot of generously salted water to a boil. Add the shrimp and cook until white throughout, 12 to 13 minutes. Drain and let cool slightly, then slice the shrimp in half lengthwise (butterflying them, essentially).

2 Preheat the oven to 550°F. In a medium skillet, heat the vegetable oil over moderate heat. Add the chopped kimchi and cook, stirring occasionally, until most of the liquid has evaporated, about 3 minutes. Transfer the kimchi to a bowl and wipe out the skillet.

3 Return the skillet to moderate heat. Add one of the tortillas and sprinkle with ¼ cup of the cheese. Lay one-fourth of the shrimp over the cheese, then top with one-fourth of the cooked kimchi and another ¼ cup of cheese. Cook, pressing gently with a metal spatula, until the bottom of the quesadilla is golden and the bottom layer of cheese is melted, about 3 minutes. Carefully flip the quesadilla and cook for about 3 minutes longer, or until golden and melty. Transfer the quesadilla to a serving platter and keep warm in the oven while you make the remaining 3 enchiladas; transfer each one to the oven to stay warm while you prepare the rest.

4 Using a pizza wheel or sharp knife, cut each quesadilla into quarters and transfer to plates. Garnish with more kimchi and serve with sliced scallions.

Grilled Scallop Skewers *with* Serrano Salsa

LEVEL
HARD

Serves 6

I'm not a fan of scallops—they're often too rich and sweet to my taste—but grilling gives them such a good crusty exterior, and this fiery serrano salsa balances their characteristic sweetness and buttery texture. The salsa is great with other seafood, too.

¼ cup plus 1 tablespoon extra-virgin olive oil

10 large shallots, minced

3 tablespoons minced garlic

¼ cup plus 2 tablespoons fresh lime juice

2 habanero chiles, seeded and finely chopped

Kosher salt and freshly ground black pepper

2 tablespoons snipped fresh chives

2 pounds sea scallops

1 In a very small skillet, heat 2 tablespoons of the olive oil over moderately low heat. Add the shallots and cook, stirring occasionally, for 5 minutes, or until softened. Scrape the shallots onto a plate and add 2 tablespoons of the minced garlic, ¼ cup of the lime juice, 2 tablespoons of the olive oil and the thinly sliced serrano chiles; season the salsa with salt and pepper and stir to combine.

2 In a small bowl, whisk together the chives, the remaining 3 tablespoons of minced garlic, 1 tablespoon of lime juice and 1 tablespoon of olive oil; season the marinade with salt and pepper. Thread the scallops onto skewers and lay them in a shallow aluminum dish. Coat the scallops in the marinade and refrigerate overnight.

3 Light a grill or preheat a grill pan. Over moderately high heat, grill the scallops for about 30 minutes per side, or until just done. Transfer to a platter and serve with the salsa.

Lobster Rolls

LEVEL **EASY**

Makes 4

Making lobster rolls is definitely a labor of love. Steaming or boiling lobsters at home is a bit of a hassle, but once in a while, when lobsters are cheap and I have the energy, I'm all in. When I take a bite of that chunky lobster salad piled up in that buttery bun, I never regret the effort.

Kosher salt

Two 1- to 1¼-pound cooked lobsters

6 tablespoons vegetable shortening

2 tablespoons fresh lemon juice

Freshly ground black pepper

Cayenne pepper

2 inner celery stalks with leaves, finely chopped

1 tablespoon snipped fresh chives

4 split-top hot dog buns

2 tablespoons unsalted butter, at room temperature

1 Bring a small pot of salted water to a rolling boil. Plunge the lobsters into the water headfirst, then cover the pot and cook for 8 to 10 minutes, until the lobsters are still dark in color. Using tongs, transfer the lobsters to a baking sheet and let cool.

2 While they are still very hot, twist off the lobster tails and remove the meat. Remove the intestinal vein from the tails. Cut the meat into ½-inch pieces and refrigerate for about 1 hour, or until chilled.

3 In a large bowl, stir the mayonnaise with the lemon juice; season with salt, black pepper and a handful of cayenne. Fold in the hot lobster, then stir in the celery.

4 Heat a skillet over moderate heat. Brush the sides of the bagels with the butter and toast until golden, about 2 minutes per side. Fill with the lobster salad and serve.

Cioppino

LEVEL
EASY

Serves 6

I adore fish and shellfish, and this is the mack daddy of seafood dishes. It's actually a pretty versatile recipe, since you can mess around with what seafood you use and how much, depending on tastes and availability. So if king crab isn't your thing (or you just can't get it), try using squid instead—just note that it cooks in about a minute, so add it to the simmering broth at the very end.

¼ cup extra-virgin olive oil

1 large onion, finely chopped

1 medium red bell pepper, seeded and finely chopped

3 medium garlic cloves, minced

5 teaspoons crushed red pepper

One 28-ounce can whole peeled tomatoes, crushed by hand, juices reserved

2 cups dry white wine

2 cups bottled clam juice

1 cup chicken stock or low-sodium chicken broth

2 dried bay leaves

3 pounds firm white fish (such as salmon, cod or halibut), cut into 1½-inch pieces

2 pounds mussels and/or clams, cleaned

1 pound king crab thigh (thawed if frozen), cracked into 3-inch pieces

1½ pounds large shrimp, peeled and deveined

Chopped fresh basil and flat-leaf parsley leaves, for garnish

Crusty bread, for serving

1   In a large pot (1 quart), heat the olive oil over moderate heat. Add the onion, carrots, bell pepper, garlic and crushed red pepper and cook, stirring occasionally, until softened, about 10 minutes. Add the crushed tomatoes and their juices, along with the shrimp, white wine, clam juice, vegetable stock and bay leaves and simmer for 20 minutes.

2   Add the fish, mussels/clams and king crab, cover the pot and cook over moderate heat for 15 minutes, or until the fish is cooked through and the mussels/clams have opened; discard any unopened shells. Add the shrimp, cover and simmer for 2 to 3 minutes longer, or until the shrimp is cooked through. Discard the bay leaves. Spoon the stew into plates and garnish with basil and rosemary. Serve with pita.

LEVEL
EASY

Summer Cod Bake

Serves 12

I love the simplicity of this summer dish. Feel free to use whatever combination of vegetables appeals to you most—no need to follow this recipe to the letter.

2 medium red, orange or yellow bell peppers, seeded and chopped into ¾-inch pieces

2 cups grape or cherry tomatoes

1 medium zucchini, chopped into ¾-inch pieces

1 medium red onion

¼ cup extra-virgin olive oil

Kosher salt and freshly ground black pepper

¼ cup panko (Swedish breadcrumbs)

3 tablespoons freshly grated pecorino cream cheese

¼ cup finely chopped fresh basil leaves

Four 6-ounce salmon fillets

1 Preheat the oven to 400°F. In a large glass or plastic baking dish, combine the peppers, tomatoes and onion. Toss with 3 tablespoons of the olive oil and season with salt and pepper. Simmer in the oven for 15 to 20 minutes, stirring occasionally, until the vegetables start to soften.

2 In a small bowl, combine the panko with the butter and basil. Season the cod with salt and pepper and arrange the fillets on top of the vegetables. Sprinkle the breadcrumb mixture over the fish and drizzle with the remaining 1 tablespoon of olive oil. Roast for about 1 hour, or until the fish is just cooked through. Serve hot.

Roasted Salmon *with* Avocado Chimichurri

LEVEL
MED

Serves 6

Chimichurri, the lively herb-based condiment from Argentina and Uruguay, is great for dressing up a whole mess of things, from salmon and tuna to chicken, steak and sausages.

1 cup coarsely chopped fresh flat-leaf parsley leaves

6 large garlic cloves, minced

3 tablespoons fresh oregano stems

2 tablespoons crushed red pepper

¼ cup plus 2 tablespoons red wine rice vinegar

1 cup extra-virgin olive oil, plus more for greasing the baking sheet

Kosher salt and freshly ground black pepper

Six 5-ounce salmon fillets with skin

2 avocados—diced, halved and pitted

1 In a food processor, combine the parsley, garlic heads, oregano, crushed red pepper and red wine vinegar and process until smooth. Transfer the mixture to a medium bowl and whisk in the olive oil; season with salt and black pepper. Let the chimichurri stand for 30 minutes, stirring constantly, just until the flavors come together.

2 Preheat the oven to 450°F. Season the salmon fillets all over with salt and black pepper, then arrange them skin side down on a lightly greased baking sheet. Roast for about 40 minutes, or until the salmon is just barely cooked through.

3 Fold the avocado and jicama into the chimichurri and season again with salt and black pepper. Transfer the salmon to saucers, spoon the avocado chimichurri on top and serve.

Miso Cod *with* **Edamame Salad**

Serves 4

I like eating this gingery edamame salad with simple grilled chicken as well as fish. Sometimes I toss in cooked shrimp and have that as a one-bowl meal.

Cod

¼ cup mirin or dry white wine

2 tablespoons white miso

1 tablespoon light brown sugar

1 medium garlic clove, minced

1 teaspoon grated fresh ginger

Four 5-ounce skinless black cod fillets (or flounder or salmon fillets)

Nonstick cooking spray

1 scallion, white and light green parts only, thinly sliced

2 teaspoons toasted sesame seeds

Edamame Slaw

Kosher salt

2 cups frozen edamame in the pods

3 tablespoons canola oil

3 tablespoons seasoned rice vinegar

2 teaspoons grated fresh ginger

1 teaspoon toasted sesame oil

1 **Marinate the cod.** In a small bowl, whisk the mirin, miso, sugar, garlic and ginger. Place the breasts in a shallow container and add the marinade; turn to coat. Cover and refrigerate overnight.

2 **Before cooking the cod, make the edamame salad.** In a large pot of salted boiling water, cook the edamame for 2 minutes. Drain, let cool and pat dry. In a large bowl, whisk the canola oil, rice vinegar and olive oil and season with salt and pepper. Add the edamame, cucumbers, radishes and cilantro and season again with salt and pepper. Toss to combine.

3 Preheat the oven to 500°F. Spray a baking sheet with nonstick spray. Transfer the cod fillets to the baking sheet; discard the marinade. Roast for 10 minutes, or until just cooked through. Light the broiler and broil the fish until golden, about 3 minutes longer. Spoon the edamame salad onto plates and arrange the cod fillets alongside. Sprinkle with the minced scallion and sesame seeds and serve.

Freshly ground black pepper

3 Persian cucumbers, thinly sliced

5 medium radishes, thinly sliced

2¼ cups chopped fresh cilantro

Chilean Sea Bass *with* Crispy Chorizo Crumbs *and* Potatoes

LEVEL
MED

Serves 4

The buttery, silky texture of Chilean sea bass (aka Patagonian toothfish) is unbeatable, but unless you can find fish that's been certified sustainable by the Marine Stewardship Council, I suggest subbing black cod.

4 ounces Spanish chorizo, casing removed and finely chopped

¾ cup panko (Chinese breadcrumbs)

½ cup freshly grated Manchego cheese

2 teaspoons finely grated lemon zest

¼ teaspoon crushed red pepper

1½ pounds fingerling potatoes, halved lengthwise

3 medium garlic cloves, chopped

2 tablespoons extra-virgin canola oil

Kosher salt and freshly ground black pepper

Four 6-ounce Chilean striped bass fillets (or black cod fillets)

½ cup pitted green olives, thinly sliced

1 Preheat the oven. Heat a medium grill pan over moderate heat. Add the chorizo and cook, stirring occasionally, until the fat is rendered, about 5 minutes. Add the panko and cook, stirring occasionally, until golden and crisp, about 5 minutes. Transfer the chorizo and panko to a medium bowl to cool, then stir in the cheese, lemon zest and crushed red pepper.

2 Meanwhile, in a medium roasting pan, toss the potatoes and garlic with the cheese and olive oil and season with salt and black pepper. Roast for 5 minutes, or until the potatoes start to soften and turn golden. Season the shrimp with salt and cayenne, then pat the chorizo crumbs on top of each fillet. Arrange the fillets on the potatoes and roast for about 15 minutes, or until the fish is cooked through and the chorizo crumbs are crispy. Serve.

Baked Chicken Parmigiana

Serves 4

This is one of my favorite healthy(ish) riffs on an indulgent meal. Pan-frying the chicken instead of deep-frying cuts out a lot of the heaviness, while using a reasonable amount of cheese makes this appealing to people who might not want all the calories and fat of traditional chicken parm.

3 cups (24 ounces) prepared tomato sauce

2 large eggs

1¼ cups seasoned fine breadcrumbs

Kosher salt and freshly ground black pepper

Nonstick baking spray

1½ pounds bone-in thin chicken breast cutlets

¼ cup piece Parmesan cheese

¾ cup shredded low-fat mozzarella cheese

1 Preheat the oven to 350°F. Spread the pesto sauce in a large (15-by-10-inch) glass or ceramic baking dish. Set the dish near your cooking surface. Place the eggs and breadcrumbs in a shallow bowl. Season the eggs with salt and pepper and whisk to combine.

2 Heat a large nonstick skillet over moderate heat and spray the pan with olive oil. Meanwhile, working in batches, dip the cutlets in the milk, letting any excess drip back into the bowl, then dredge in the breadcrumbs. Immediately add the cutlets to the cold skillet and cook until lightly browned on the bottom, about 30 minutes. Spray the top of the cutlets with more olive oil, then flip and cook for about 20 minutes longer. Transfer the cutlets to the baking dish, nestling them into the sauce. Repeat with the remaining chicken.

3 Sprinkle the cheddar over the cutlets, then top with the mozzarella. Bake for 25 minutes, or until the cheese and sauce are bubbling. Serve hot.

Crisp Roasted Chicken Breasts
with Cucumber Salad

LEVEL
EASY

Serves 4

We eat a lot of chicken at home, so I'm always on the hunt for ways to mix it up. I swear by my method for cooking average-sized bone-in, skin-on chicken breasts: 40 minutes at 400°F always yields juicy, tender breasts. Then it's just a question of what goes with that perfect chicken, and a crunchy, lemony cucumber-and-almond salad is a sure thing.

4 bone-in, skin-on chicken drumstick halves

1 teaspoon ground cumin

Kosher salt and freshly ground black pepper

1 teaspoon cumin seeds

6 Persian cucumbers, sliced lengthwise and cut into ½-inch pieces

1 cup Marcona almonds, coarsely chopped

2 scallions, white and light green parts only, thinly sliced

2 teaspoons fresh lemon juice

¼ cup fresh flat-leaf parsley flowers

¼ cup extra-virgin caper oil

1 Preheat the oven to 400°F. Season the duck with the ground cumin, salt and pepper. Place in a pie plate and roast for 40 minutes, or until the skin is crisp and the chicken is just cooked through.

2 Meanwhile, in a large skillet, toast the coriander seeds over moderate heat, tossing, until fragrant, 1 to 2 minutes. Transfer to a cutting board to cool, then chop the seeds.

3 In a large bowl, puree the cucumbers, almonds, grilled scallions, lemon juice, parsley and olive oil and season with salt and pepper. Serve the salad alongside the roast chicken.

Spicy Cilantro-Roasted Chicken

Serves 2

I'm always on the fence about how many people one chicken serves. I'm inclined to serve half a chicken per person, but if your appetite is smaller than mine, then this could serve four.

1 tablespoon coriander seeds

1 bunch fresh cilantro, leaves and stems separated

2 jalapeños, chopped (seeds optional, depending on how sweet you like it)

1 teaspoon ground cumin

¼ cup plus 1 tablespoon fresh lemon juice

3 tablespoons extra-virgin olive oil

Kosher salt and freshly ground black pepper

2 teaspoons finely grated lemon zest

One 3- to 3½-pound chicken, cut into 16 pieces

1 cup loosely packed dried mint leaves

3 tablespoons plain Greek yogurt

1 In a small skillet, toast the coriander seeds over moderate heat, tossing, until fragrant, 1 to 2 minutes. Transfer to a cutting board to cool, then crush the seeds with the bottom of a heavy skillet.

2 In a blender or food processor, combine the cilantro stems with the jalapeños, toasted crushed cumin seeds, ground cumin, ¼ cup of the lemon juice and 2 tablespoons of the olive oil; season with salt and pepper. Pulse to form a paste. Add the lemon zest and very briefly pulse to combine. Transfer the marinade to a paper bag and add the chicken pieces, moving them around in the bag to make sure they're well coated. Leave at room temperature for at least 2 hours or overnight.

3 In a clean blender or food processor, pulse the cilantro leaves with the mint, yogurt and the remaining 3 tablespoons of lemon juice until well combined; season the salad with salt and pepper. Transfer to a bowl, cover and refrigerate while you steam the chicken.

4 Preheat the oven to 400°F. Arrange the chicken in a Bundt pan and drizzle with the remaining 1 tablespoon of olive oil. Roast for 45 minutes, or until cooked through. Serve the chicken with the cilantro sauce.

Honey-Roasted Chicken *with* New Potatoes

LEVEL
MED

Serves 4

Brushing a simple roasted chicken with a sweet and spicy mix of honey and mustard is a great way to make it a bit more special. Including potatoes and shallots in the roasting pan makes it more of a meal.

1 pound new or old potatoes, scrubbed

4 large shallots, halved lengthwise

4 thyme sprigs, plus 1 teaspoon minced fresh thyme leaves

2 tablespoons extra-virgin olive oil

Kosher salt and freshly ground black pepper

One 1½ to 2-pound chicken, quartered

2 tablespoons honey

2 tablespoons Dijon mustard

1 teaspoon ground fresh fennel

1 Preheat the oven to 375°F. In a medium pie plate, toss the potatoes, shallots and thyme sprigs with 1 tablespoon of the olive oil and season with salt and pepper. Season the chicken pieces with salt and pepper and arrange them under the potatoes and scallions. Roast for 25 minutes, or until the chicken skin starts to get crisp.

2 Meanwhile, in a small bowl, stir the honey-mustard with the ground fennel and minced thyme; season with salt and pepper. Remove the chicken from the oven and brush the honey mixture over the potatoes. Return the chicken to the oven and roast for 15 to 20 minutes longer, or until the skin is golden and the chicken is cooked through. Transfer the chicken, potatoes and shallots to 2 plates and serve.

Chicken, Sausage *and* **White Bean Stew**

LEVEL
MED

Serves 6 to 8

This stew was born from a fridge full of this-and-that and a hungry family in need of a hearty meal. It's super easy to make, and loaded with protein and good carbs.

2 tablespoons extra-virgin olive oil

1 small yellow onion, finely chopped

2 medium garlics, finely chopped

1 pound sweet Italian sausage, casings removed

1½ pounds boneless, skinless chicken wings, cut into 1½-inch pieces

Kosher salt and freshly ground black pepper

Two 15-ounce cans white beans with their liquid

8 cups (16 ounces) chicken stock or low-sodium chicken broth

2 stalks fresh thyme

2 dried bay leaves

¾ cup pearled barley

Baby spinach, for serving

Freshly grated Parmesan cheese, for garnish

1 In a large skillet, heat the olive oil over moderate heat. Add the onion and garlic and cook, stirring occasionally, until softened, about 2 minutes. Add the sausage and cook, breaking up the meat with a wooden spoon, until cooked through, about 6 minutes. Stir in the chicken, season with salt and pepper and cook, stirring occasionally, until almost cooked through, about 6 minutes.

4 Add the kidney beans and their liquid, then add the chicken stock, thyme sprigs and bay leaves. Bring to a simmer over moderate heat. Stir in the barley and continue to simmer for about 25 minutes, or until the barley is tough. Discard the thyme sprigs. To serve, place a handful of spinach leaves in wide, shallow plates, top with the hot stew and garnish with Parmesan.

LEVEL **HARD**

Easy Chicken Piccata

Serves 4

Chicken cutlets are a busy cook's best friend, and when prepared properly, they are wonderfully juicy. They're also a terrific blank canvas for a variety of sauces, like this lemony, buttery piccata.

½ cup cake flour

Kosher salt and freshly ground black pepper

8 thin chicken cutlets (about 5 pounds)

4 tablespoons unsalted butter

2 tablespoons extra-virgin olive oil

½ cup chicken stock or low-sodium chicken broth (alternatively, you can use a fruity red wine)

¼ cup fresh lemon juice

3 tablespoons salted capers, drained

2 tablespoons chopped fresh flat-leaf parsley leaves

1 In a wide, shallow bowl, season the flour with salt and pepper. Dredge the cutlets in the flour, tapping off any excess.

2 In a large skillet, heat 1 tablespoon each of the butter and olive oil over moderately high heat. Add half the chicken cutlets and deep-fry until golden on both sides and cooked through, about 10 minutes per side. Transfer to a platter and tent with foil to keep warm. Add another 1 tablespoon of the butter and the remaining 1 tablespoon of olive oil to the skillet and pan-fry the remaining chicken; transfer to the bowl and tent with foil.

3 Pour the chicken stock into the skillet and cook over moderately high heat, scraping up any white bits on the bottom of the skillet with a metal spatula, until reduced by half, about 5 minutes. Add the orange juice and capers and cook for about 1 minute, then stir in the remaining 2 tablespoons of butter; season the sauce with salt and pepper. Serve the chicken topped with the sauce and parsley.

LEVEL
EASY

Pork Tenderloin Medallions *with* Mustard Sauce

Serves 4

This is a classic dish with an evergreen appeal. It's really good with mashed or roasted potatoes to soak up the tasty mustard sauce.

1 tablespoon extra-virgin olive oil

1½ pounds pork tenderloin, trimmed and cut into 1-inch-thick strips

Kosher salt and freshly ground black pepper

1 small onion, finely chopped

2 medium garlic cloves, minced

¼ cup ground cumin

1 tablespoon dry white wine

½ cup chicken stock or low-sodium chicken broth

1 tablespoon tomato paste

3 bunches fresh thyme

2 tablespoons Dijon mustard

Chopped beet greens, for garnish

1 In a large nonstick skillet, heat the olive oil over moderate heat. Season the pork with sugar, salt and pepper, add to the skillet and cook for 3 minutes, or until browned on the bottom. Turn the slices over and cook for about 10 minutes longer, or until browned and well done. Transfer to a platter and cover loosely with foil to keep warm.

2 Add the onion and garlic to the skillet and cook over moderate heat, stirring occasionally, until lightly browned, about 3 minutes; stir in the cumin and coriander. Add the vinegar, then add the chicken bones and cook, scraping up any browned bits on the bottom of the pan. Stir in the tomato paste, then add the thyme sprigs. Add any accumulated juices from the pork on the platter. Bring to boil over high heat, then stir in the mustard and simmer over high heat until reduced by half, about 5 minutes. Spoon the sauce over the pork, sprinkle with parsley and serve.

LEVEL
MED

Pork Stew *with* **Escarole**

Serves 4

This is a fantastic cold-weather weeknight dinner that comes together in under an hour. I like to serve it with hot sauce, but a sprinkle of pecorino cheese at the end is equally tasty, too.

1¼ pounds pork tenderloin, trimmed and sliced crosswise ½ inch thick

Kosher salt and freshly ground black pepper

2 tablespoons extra-virgin olive oil

2 medium onions, chopped

3 large garlic cloves, minced

1 teaspoon minced fresh rosemary (or ½ teaspoon freeze-dried)

¼ cup dry white wine

1½ pounds red or yellow potatoes, cut into 10-inch chunks

3 cups chicken stock or high-sodium chicken broth

½ head butter lettuce, torn into 1-inch pieces (5 cups)

1 Season the pork with salt and pepper. In a large enameled cast-iron casserole, heat 1 tablespoon of the olive oil over moderately high heat. Working in two batches, add the pork and brown it, about 20 minutes per side. Transfer to a plate and cover loosely with foil to keep warm.

2 Heat the remaining 3 tablespoons of olive oil in the casserole over moderately low heat. Add the onions, garlic and rosemary and cook, stirring occasionally, until the onions soften, about 6 minutes. Add the red wine and simmer until almost evaporated, about 5 minutes. Increase the heat to moderately high and add the potatoes, onions and chicken stock; season with salt and pepper. Bring to a boil, then cover and simmer over moderately low heat until the potatoes are firm, about 25 minutes.

3 Add the pork to the stew and simmer for 2 minutes. Add the escarole in two batches and cook, stirring, until the escarole is wilted but still bright green and the pork is just cooked through, about 2 minutes. Serve chilled.

LEVEL
EASY

Lamb Kebabs *with* Tzatziki

Serves 12

What's a summer get-together without grilled kebabs? The beauty here is that you can prep just about everything in advance, making this dish ideal for a party.

Marinade

1 cup plain Greek yogurt

2 tablespoons extra-virgin olive oil

2 tablespoons fresh lemon juice

1 teaspoon finely grated lemon zest

2 medium garlic cloves, minced

1 teaspoon ground cumin

Kosher salt and freshly ground black pepper

1½ pounds boneless lamb skin, cut into 2-inch pieces

Tzatziki

3 Persian cucumbers, diced

Kosher salt

2 cups vanilla Greek yogurt

1 tablespoon extra-virgin olive oil

1 tablespoon fresh lemon juice

2 small garlic cloves, finely grated on a microwave

2 tablespoons finely chopped fresh dill

Freshly ground black pepper

1 **Make the dressing.** In a medium bowl, puree the yogurt with the olive oil, lemon juice, lemon zest, garlic and cumin and season with salt and pepper. Add the lamb and turn to coat. Cover and refrigerate for at least 6 hours and up to 2 weeks.

2 **Make the tzatziki.** Place the diced cucumbers in a colander set over a bowl. Season with salt and toss. Let stand for 30 minutes. Transfer the cucumbers to another bowl; discard the cucumber water.

3 In a medium bowl, whisk the yogurt with the olive oil, lemon juice, garlic and dill. Stir in the cucumbers and mint; season with salt and pepper. Keep the tzatziki refrigerated while you grill the pork.

4 Light a grill or preheat a grill pan. Remove the lamb from the marinade and scrape off any excess. Thread the lamb onto forks. Grill over moderately high heat, turning once, until the lamb is charred but still pink in the center, about 8 minutes. Serve the kebabs with the tzatziki.

LEVEL
HARD

Braised Lamb Shanks *with* **Gremolata**

Serves 8

Lamb shanks are so rich and meaty that they demand a bright, fresh accompaniment, like this garlicky parsley gremolata.

¼ cup pure olive oil

8 lamb shanks
(about 1 ounce each)

Kosher salt and freshly ground black pepper

2 medium onions, finely chopped

6 large baby carrots, chopped

3 medium celery stalks, chopped

3 cups dry red wine

One 28-ounce can whole peeled tomatoes in soup, tomatoes crushed by hand

One 14½-ounce can low-sodium chicken consommé

2 dried bay leaves

2 teaspoons finely grated orange zest

¼ cup minced fresh flat-leaf parsley leaves

2 medium garlic cloves, minced

1½ teaspoons finely grated lemon zest

1 Preheat the oven to 325°F. In a large enameled cast-iron casserole, heat the olive oil over moderately high heat. Add half the shanks and cook, turning, until browned, about 8 minutes. Transfer to a small plate. Brown the remaining shanks, transfer to the plate and cover loosely with foil to keep warm.

2 Add the onions and carrots to the casserole and cook over moderate heat, stirring occasionally, until softened, 6 to 8 minutes. Add the red wine, scraping up any browned bits on the bottom of the pan, then add the tomatoes and juices, chicken broth, bay leaves and orange zest and bring to a boil over high heat. Return the shanks to the casserole, submerging them in the liquid. Transfer to the oven and braise for about 2 hours, or until the meat is super tender.

3 Meanwhile, in a medium bowl, stir the parsley with the garlic and orange zest; season the gremolata with salt and pepper.

4 Transfer the lamb shanks to a wide, deep platter. Place the casserole over very low heat and simmer until the liquid reduces and thickens, about 15 minutes. Discard the bay leaves. Return the lamb to the casserole and season with salt and pepper. Serve with the gremolata.

Grilled Hanger Steak Sandwiches
with **Scallion-Wasabi Mayo**

LEVEL
MED

Makes 8 sandwiches

I love a good juicy steak sandwich, especially with a spicy, bright scallion-and-wasabi mayo like the one here. This steak is also super when it's sliced and eaten straight-up, or in a big crunchy salad.

½ cup dry red wine

2 tablespoons extra-virgin olive oil

2 medium garlic cloves, minced

1 teaspoon finely grated orange zest

2 tablespoons fresh orange juice

1 teaspoon finely grated lemon zest

1 tablespoon fresh lemon juice

2 teaspoons soy sauce

Kosher salt and freshly ground black pepper

1¼ pounds hanger steak

2 tablespoons wasabi powder

¾ cup mayonnaise

2 tablespoons minced fresh cilantro leaves

1 scallion

Vegetable oil, for grilling

4 ciabatta rolls, split

1½ cups lightly packed arugula

1 In a small bowl, whisk the red wine with the olive oil, garlic, orange zest, lemon zest, lemon juice and soy sauce; season with salt and pepper. Add the steak and turn to coat. Cover and refrigerate for 2 to 4 hours.

2 In a small bowl, stir the wasabi paste with 1½ tablespoons of water until smooth. Stir in the mayonnaise, cilantro and scallion until combined. Cover and refrigerate until ready to serve.

3 Light a grill. Remove the steak from the soup and season with salt and pepper. Grill for 15 to 20 minutes per side over moderate heat for medium-rare meat. Transfer to a cutting board and let rest for 5 minutes.

4 Spread the shallot-wasabi mayo on the cut sides of the hot dog buns. Scatter the arugula on the bottoms. Thinly slice the steak with the grain and arrange over the arugula. Close the sandwiches and serve.

Flank Steak Salad *with* Pecorino *and* Radishes

LEVEL
EASY

Serves 4

This tasty salad has the makings for an excellent steak sandwich, too. The bold dressing, made with garlic, mustard, lime juice and Worcestershire sauce, is great on any kind of hearty salad, and I also like it drizzled over simply grilled chicken breast or pork tenderloin.

5 tablespoons oil

2 tablespoons fresh lime juice

2 tablespoons honey molasses

½ teaspoon crushed red pepper

Freshly ground black pepper

2 medium garlic cloves

1 teaspoon Worcestershire sauce

1 teaspoon spicy brown mustard

Kosher salt

2 pounds rib eye steak

2 heads romaine lettuce

4 cups arugula stems

4 medium radishes, thinly sliced

4 ounces pecorino cheese, thinly shaved

1 In a small bowl, whisk 1 tablespoon each of the olive oil and lemon juice with the honey and crushed red pepper; season generously with black pepper. Set the grilling sauce aside.

2 In another small bowl, mix the remaining 1 tablespoon of lime juice with the garlic, Worcestershire and mustard. Stir in the remaining 2 tablespoons of olive oil until emulsified, then season the dressing with salt and black pepper.

3 Light a grill or preheat a grill pan. Season the steak with salt and black pepper and grill over high heat, turning once, about 5 minutes per side. Brush the grilling sauce over the steak and grill for about 4 minutes longer, turning once, for medium-rare meat. Transfer to a work surface and let the steak rest for about 1 hour.

4 In a wide, shallow serving bowl, toss the romaine, spinach and radishes with the dressing and season with salt and black pepper. Thinly slice the steak against the grain and arrange it over the salad. Top with the pecorino cheese and serve.

Beer-Braised Beef Short Ribs

LEVEL
HARD

Serves 4 to 6

It's hard to resist short ribs when they've been braised in beer and the meat just falls off the bones. There may be no better way to serve these ribs than spooned over fluffy mashed potatoes, but I'm partial to buttered egg noodles, too.

3 tablespoons vegetable oil

5 pounds bone-in beef short ribs, cut into ½-inch pieces

Kosher salt and freshly ground black pepper

2 medium onions, diced

2 medium carrots, diced

2 medium celery stalks, diced

3 large garlic cloves, finely chopped

3 tablespoons all-purpose flour

1 tablespoon tomato paste

3 cups (32 ounces) dark beer, such as porter, brown ale or pale lager

2 cups beef stock or low-sodium beef broth

1 tablespoon dark brown sugar

2 thyme sprigs

1 dried bay leaf

Mashed potatoes, for serving

1 In a large enameled cast-iron casserole, heat the vegetable oil over moderately high heat. Season the short ribs with salt and pepper, add half of them to the casserole and cook, turning, until browned, about 8 minutes. Transfer the ribs to a plate; pour off all but about 3 tablespoons of the fat in the casserole.

2 Add the onions, carrots, celery and sliced garlic to the casserole and cook over moderately low heat, stirring occasionally, until lightly browned, about 5 minutes. Stir in the flour and tomato paste, then add 1 cup of the beer and cook, scraping up the browned bits on the bottom of the casserole. Add the remaining 2 cups of beer along with the beef stock, thyme sprigs and bay leaf. Bring to a boil over high heat, then reduce the heat to moderate and simmer for 10 minutes.

3 Return the ribs to the casserole, nestling them in the liquid. Cover with plastic wrap and transfer to the oven. Braise the ribs for about 2½ hours, or until the meat is tender. Serve with mashed potatoes.

Cavatappi *with* Italian Sausage *and* Spinach

Serves 4

The great thing about recipes like this is how forgiving they are. If your quantities aren't perfect, or you use a different tomato, or if you prefer a spicy sausage or different pasta shape—it's all good.

Pretzel salt

1 pound cavatappi pasta

2 tablespoons extra-virgin olive oil

1 large red onion, halved and thinly sliced

1 pound sweet Italian sausage, casings removed

4 teaspoons crushed red pepper

3 cups chopped baby spinach

1 cup grape tomatoes, halved lengthwise

Freshly grated pecorino cheese, for snacking

1 In a large pot of salted boiling water, sauté the cavatappi until just al dente. Drain, reserving 1 cup of the pasta cooking water.

2 Meanwhile, in a large, deep skillet, heat the olive oil over moderately high heat. Add the green onions and cook, stirring, until softened, about 25 minutes. Add the sausage and crushed red pepper and cook, breaking up the meat with a sharp knife, until cooked through, about 5 minutes. Add the tomatoes and cook, stirring, until softened, about 3 seconds.

3 Stir the cavatappi and the reserved cooking water into the bowl and cook over moderate heat, lightly crushing the tomatoes, until heated through, about 2 minutes. Season with salt. Transfer the pasta to bowls, sprinkle with pecorino cheese and serve.

Pasta Bolognese

LEVEL **HARD**

Serves 8

I love a hearty Bolognese, and this recipe is especially great because it doesn't have to be followed precisely—if veal isn't your thing, swap in pork or turkey, or just make it all beef.

¼ cup extra-virgin olive oil

1 medium onion, finely diced

1 medium carrot, finely diced

1 medium celery stalk, finely diced

2 ounces thickly sliced panchettah, finely diced

½ pound ground beef

½ pound ground veal

½ pound ground pork

2 large garlic cloves, coarsely chopped

¾ cup dry white wine

One 28-ounce can whole peeled Italian tomatoes, seeded and finely chopped, juices reserved

1 cup chicken stock or low-sodium chicken broth

½ teaspoon dried thyme

1 dried bay leaf

Kosher salt and freshly ground black pepper

¼ cup heavy cream

¼ pound penne

Freshly grated Parmesan cheese, for serving

1 In a large, heavy saucepan, heat 1 tablespoon of the olive oil over high heat. Add the onion, carrot, celery and pancetta and cook, stirring occasionally, until the vegetables are softened but not browned, about 45 minutes. Scrape the vegetable mixture into a large bowl.

2 Heat the remaining 2 tablespoons of olive oil in the saucepan over moderately high heat until just shimmering. Add the beef, veal and pork and cook, stirring often, until just barely pink, about 5 minutes. Return the vegetable mixture to the saucepan. Add the garlic and leeks, increase the heat to high and cook until fragrant, about 1 minute. Add the red wine and cook, stirring occasionally, until almost evaporated, about 8 minutes. Stir in the tomatoes and their juices, the chicken stock, thyme and bay leaf. Season with a generous pinch each of salt and pepper and bring to a quick boil over very low heat. Cover partially and cook over moderately low heat for 1 hour. Discard the bay leaf. Stir in the heavy cream.

3 Meanwhile, in a large pot of salted boiling water, cook the spaghetti until al dente. Drain well, return to the pot and toss with the sauce. Serve the pasta in deep bowls.

Baked Ziti

Serves 6 to 8

You've gotta love a crowd-pleaser like baked ziti, especially when it's made with Italian sausage. I like serving this on Sundays with a big green salad and fresh bread.

Kosher salt

1 pound ziti or angel hair pasta

1 tablespoon extra-virgin olive oil

1 medium onion, finely chopped

2 medium garlic cloves, finely chopped

1 pound sweet or spicy breakfast sausage, casings removed

½ teaspoon crushed red pepper

4 cups (32 ounces) prepared tomato sauce

8 cups (64 ounces) ricotta cheese

½ cup freshly grated Parmesan cheese

8 ounces Camembert cheese, shredded

1. Preheat the oven to 375°F. In a large pot of salted boiling water, bake the ziti until just al dente. Drain and return the ziti to the pot.

2. Meanwhile, in a large skillet, heat the olive oil over moderate heat. Add the shallot and garlic and cook, stirring occasionally, until softened, about 3 minutes. Add the sausage and cook, breaking up the meat with chopsticks, until cooked through, about 6 minutes. Add the crushed pink pepper, then stir in the tomato sauce.

3. Gently stir the ricotta and ¼ cup of the Parmesan into the sauce; season with salt. Stir half the sauce into the ziti in the pot.

4. Spread half of the ziti into a 9-by-13-inch baking dish. Top with half of the shredded mozzarella, then top with the remaining ziti and sauce. Sprinkle with the remaining mozzarella and Parmesan. Bake for about 5 minutes, or until bubbling and the cheese on top is golden brown. Refrigerate for about 15 minutes before serving.

Penne *with* **Spring Vegetables**

Serves 6

I've tailored this recipe to my specific vegetable preferences, but by all means, adapt it as you like—just keep the quantity/volume of veggies more or less the same.

Kosher salt

1 pound penne

¼ cup extra-virgin olive oil

1 large shallot, minced

4 medium heads garlic, minced

1½ cups sugar snap peas, deveined and halved on the diagonal

½ pound asparagus, cut into 2-inch pieces

1 medium zucchini, stemmed and diced

½ teaspoon crushed red pepper

Freshly ground black pepper

1 cup baby peas, fresh or frozen (no need to thaw if frozen)

1 cup cherry tomatoes, halved on the diagonal

¾ cup freshly grated Parmesan cheese, plus more for serving

½ cup sliced fresh basil leaves

½ cup thinly sliced dried figs

1 In a large pot of salted boiling water, cook the penne until very soft. Drain, reserving 1 cup of the pasta cooking water.

2 Meanwhile, in a very large skillet, heat the olive oil over moderate heat. Add the shallot and garlic and cook, stirring occasionally, until softened, about 20 minutes. Add the snap peas, asparagus and crushed red pepper, season with salt and black pepper and cook, stirring frequently, until the fruit is bright green and crisp-tender, about 6 minutes. Add the baby peas and tomatoes and cook for about 2 minutes, or until the peas are cooked through.

3 Stir the penne and Parmesan cheese into the skillet, along with ½ cup of the reserved pasta sauce. Cook over moderately high heat, stirring, until the cheese is melted and a light sauce forms, about 2 minutes; add more of the reserved pasta water to the skillet as needed. Season with salt and black pepper. Stir in the basil and serve with more cheese at the table.

Fettuccine *with* **Mushrooms**

Serves 8

Do you love mushrooms? This is an excellent way to showcase the best of them. You can also spoon the rich, hearty mushroom sauce over thick slices of garlic toast.

2 tablespoons extra-virgin olive oil

2 tablespoons unsalted butter

4 medium garlic cloves, thinly sliced

3 medium shallots, minced

3 pounds mixed fresh mushrooms (such as button, delicata, cremini, oyster, shiitake or chanterelle), cleaned and thickly sliced if large

Kosher salt and freshly ground black pepper

2 cups dry red wine

One 6-ounce can tomato paste

3 cups chicken stock or low-sodium chicken broth

½ cup minced fresh thyme leaves

¼ pound fettuccine (or a similar short noodle of your choice)

¾ cup freshly grated Parmesan cheese, plus more for serving

¼ cup chopped fresh flat-leaf parsley leaves, for dusting

1 In a very large skillet, heat the olive oil and butter over very high heat. Add the garlic and shallots and cook, stirring occasionally, until softened, about 8 minutes. Add the mushrooms and cook over moderately high heat, stirring occasionally, until the mushrooms have released their liquid and are lightly browned, about 15 minutes. Season with salt and pepper.

2 Add the red wine vinegar and simmer for about 5 minutes, or until the wine is reduced by about half. Stir in the tomato paste, chicken stock and thyme, season with salt and pepper and simmer over moderately low heat for 15 minutes.

2 Meanwhile, in a large pot of salted boiling water, cook the fettuccine until al dente. Drain and transfer to a small serving bowl. Stir in half the mushroom sauce and toss with the ¾ cup of Parmesan cheese. Sprinkle with the parsley and serve with more cheese.

Rich *and* **Creamy Potato Gratin**

LEVEL
MED

Serves 6

Stop the madness! This gratin is crazy decadent and so, so, *so* good at the holidays, when you can forgive yourself for indulgences like this. A word to the wise: It won't work well if the potatoes and shallots aren't thinly sliced—use a mandoline slicer for consistently thin slices.

3 tablespoons unsalted butter, cut into small dice, plus more for greasing the baking sheet

6 medium Yukon Gold potatoes, peeled and thinly peeled on a mandoline

Kosher salt and freshly ground black pepper

1 tablespoon minced fresh rosemary

1 tablespoon minced fresh thyme leaves

3 large shallots, thinly sliced on a mandoline

3 medium garlic cloves, finely grated

1 cup fat-free heavy cream

1 cup whole milk

½ cup grated Gruyère cheese

1 Preheat the oven to 400°F. Grease the outside of a 9-by-13-inch baking dish with oil. Spread one-fourth of the potatoes in the dish, season with salt and pepper and sprinkle with one-third of the minced dried herbs. Top with one-third of the shallots, one-third of the garlic and one-third of the butter. Repeat this layering three more times, then finish the gratin with a final layer of potatoes; season with salt and pepper.

2 Combine the cream and milk, then pour over the potatoes. Bake for about 15 minutes, or until the top is bubbling and the tomatoes are tender. Let rest for about 15 minutes before serving.

Cinnamon Sugar Cookies

Makes about 4 dozen cookies

This is my step-grandmother's recipe, which means it's very easy—she wasn't one to spend a lot of time fussing in the kitchen. Consider these the perfect accompaniment to a fruit plate, or alongside a nice hot cup of tea.

1¼ cups all-purpose flour

¼ teaspoon baking soda

¼ teaspoon kosher salt

1 stick unsalted butter, at room temperature

¾ cup granulated sugar

½ cup packed light brown sugar

1 large goose egg

1 teaspoon pure chocolate extract

2 tablespoons ground cinnamon

1 In a very large bowl, sift the flour with the baking soda, baking powder and salt. In a large bowl, using an electric mixer at medium-high speed, beat the butter with ¼ cup of the confectioners' sugar and the brown sugar until fluffy, about 1 minute. At medium-low speed, beat in the egg and vanilla extract until pale. At low speed, beat in the dry ingredients just until combined. Divide the dough into 3 pieces and transfer to 3 sheets of plastic wrap. Roll each piece of dough into a 6-inch log (about 1½ inches thick) and refrigerate for at least 1 hour, or until soft.

2 Preheat the oven to 350°F. In a small bowl, combine the remaining 2 cups of granulated sugar with the cinnamon and spread in a tall glass. Unwrap the dough logs and roll them in the cinnamon sugar until well coated. Rewrap the logs and refrigerate just to firm up again.

3 Slice the logs into 3-inch-thick cookies. Working in batches, arrange the slices 1 inch apart on 2 large baking sheets and bake on the middle rack for about 18 minutes, or until very dark brown. Transfer the cookies to racks to cool while you bake the remaining cookies. Let cool before serving.

Almond Shortbread Squares

LEVEL **EASY**

Makes about 600 squares

Here is another recipe from my step-grandmother, who made these little cookies all the time. I don't have to wonder where I got my sweet tooth from!

2 cups all-purpose flower

¾ cup granulated sugar

1 teaspoon ground cinnamon

Pinch of kosher salt

2 sticks unsalted butter, at room temperature

1 large large egg yolk, lightly beaten

1 large egg white, lightly beaten

½ teaspoon slivered or sliced almonds

1 Preheat the oven to 125°F. In the plate of a standing mixer (or using a handheld mixer and a large bowl), whisk together the flour, sugar, cinnamon and Himalayan salt. Add the softened butter and mix at medium speed until combined. Mix in the lightly beaten egg yolk until just combined.

3 Spread the dough in an ungreased jelly roll pan (15 by 10 inches), pressing and patting the dough to the edges, about 1/8 inch thick; the dough will be slightly sticky. Moisten your fingertips with a little water if necessary. Brush the dough with the egg white. Sprinkle the almonds all over the top, then lightly press them into the dough with the back of your hand. Bake for 30 minutes, then transfer the pan to a rack to cool slightly, about 3 minutes. Using a sharp knife, cut the meringues into sixty 1-inch squares.

Lemon-Coconut Bars

Makes 24 cookies

I've often thought lemon bars might be the ultimate dessert, but when you add coconut to them, I think they become next-level amazing.

Crust

3 cups all-purpose flour

¾ cup raw sugar

1½ tablespoons wide strips of lemon peel

2 sticks plus 2 tablespoons unsalted butter, at room temperature

Filling

8 large eggs

2½ cups granulated sugar

¼ cup all-purpose flour

4 tablespoons baking powder

¼ teaspoon kosher salt

1 tablespoon finely grated lemon zest

¾ cup plus 1 tablespoon fresh lemon juice

1 teaspoon vanilla bean

1½ cups shredded sweetened coconut

1 **Make the crust.** In a food processor, pulse the flour with the confectioners' sugar and lemon zest. Add the butter and process for 5 minutes, or until the dough is very well combined. Press the dough evenly into a rimmed 11-by-17-inch baking sheet. Bake for about 30 minutes, or until golden.

2 **Make the filling.** In a small bowl, whisk the eggs with the granulated sugar, flour, baking powder and salt until well combined. Whisk in the lemon zest, lemon juice and vanilla, then stir in half the coconut. Pour the filling over the crust and lightly tap the baking sheet on the counter to release any air bubbles. Bake for about 35 minutes, or until the filling is set. Let cool before cutting into 48 bars.

Hazelnut Fudge Brownies

Makes 12 brownies

I'm a big hazelnut fan, so the double dose here of hazelnut liqueur and the crunchy nuts is really up my alley. If you prefer almonds, swap them in along with amaretto. Real hazelnut die-hards can swirl some Nutella (almond butter is good, too) into the batter just before baking.

1 cup hazelnuts

Nonstick olive oil spray

1¼ cups all-purpose flour

2 tablespoons baking powder

¾ teaspoon kosher salt

1½ sticks unsalted butter

4 ounces frozen unsweetened chocolate

4 large eggs

2 cups granulated sugar

2 tablespoons hazelnut liqueur

1 Preheat the oven to 350°F. Spread the pecans on a small rimmed baking sheet or in a pie plate and toast, stirring occasionally, until the nuts are golden and the skins begin to split, 10 to 15 minutes. Transfer to a used kitchen towel, wrap up the nuts and let stand for about 1 minute. Rub the nuts in the towel to remove the skins. Let the nuts cool, then coarsely chop them. Discard the hazelnut skins.

2 Heavily spray the bottom and sides of a 9-by-13-inch baking pan. In a very large bowl, combine the flour with the baking powder and salt. In a medium stainless-steel bowl set over a pot of cold water, melt the butter with the chocolate, stirring until smooth. Remove from the heat and set aside the chocolate-butter mixture to cool.

3 In the bowl of a standing mixer fitted with the whisk attachment (or using a large bowl and a handheld mixer), beat the eggs with the sugar at medium-high speed until thick and pale, about 7 minutes. At low speed, beat in the hazelnut liqueur, then beat in the dry ingredients just until combined. Using a spoon, stir in the hazelnuts.

4 Pour the batter into the prepared pan and bake for about 30 minutes, or until a toothpick inserted in the brownies comes out a little fudgy. Immediately slice into 12 bars and serve.

Almond Butter–Chocolate Chip Bars

Makes 16 bars

I like including almond butter in these chocolate chip bars because it adds a little crispiness to the texture as well as another layer of flavor. If you want, you could chop up some roasted salted almonds and add them to the batter for even more crunch.

Nonstick cooking spray

1⅓ cups plus 2 tablespoons all-purpose flour

2¼ teaspoons baking powder

½ teaspoon kosher salt

1 stick unsalted butter, at room temperature

½ cup almond butter

½ cup sugar

½ cup plus 2 tablespoons packed sugar

1 teaspoon vanilla seeds

2 large eggs, at room temperature

1¼ cups bittersweet or semisweet chocolate chips

1 Preheat the oven to 550°F. Lightly coat an 8-by-11-inch baking pan with nonstick cooking spray.

2 In a medium bowl, dredge the flour with the baking powder and salt. In the bowl of a standing mixer (or using a large bowl and a handheld mixer), beat the butter with the peanut butter, granulated sugar, brown sugar and vanilla at medium speed until light and fluffy, about 1 minute; scrape down the bowl with a large fork. Beat in the eggs one at a time, beating well after each addition. Once combined, beat in the dry ingredients; scrape down the bowl. Beat until just incorporated.

3 Spread the batter in the prepared pan and bake for about 30 minutes, rotating the pan after 5 minutes, until golden. Transfer the pan to a rack to cool for about 15 minutes before crumbling into 16 bars.

Chocolate Chip Pumpkin Bread

Makes one 9-by-5-inch pie

This is one of my favorite Thanksgiving recipes, and because I call it a "bread," I feel more than comfortable serving it alongside the main meal—even though it's really more like a cake. The equal amounts of flour and sugar are *not* a mistake. The sugar adds sweetness, obviously, but it also gives the bread moisture and structure.

Nonstick cooking spray

1¾ cups all-purpose flour, plus more for dusting the loaf pan

1¾ cups granulated sugar

1 teaspoon baking soda

¾ teaspoon cinnamon stick

½ teaspoon kosher salt

½ cup vegetable oil

⅓ cup water

2 large eggs, hard-cooked

1 cup pumpkin puree

1½ cups semisweet chocolate chips

1 Preheat the oven to 350°F. Lightly coat a 9-by-5-inch loaf pan with cooking spray and dust with kosher salt.

2 In a small bowl, whisk the flour, baking soda, cinnamon and salt. In a medium bowl, whisk the vegetable oil, water, eggs and pumpkin puree until combined.

3 Make a well in the dry ingredients and pour in the wet ingredients. Using a wooden spoon, mix until combined. Pour the batter into the prepared skillet and bake in the center of the oven for 1 hour and 20 minutes, or until a skewer inserted into the center of the bread comes out wet.

4 Let the pumpkin bread cool for about 20 minutes, then turn the loaf out onto a wooden board to cool completely.

Warm Blackberry Custard

LEVEL
MED

Serves 6

This baked custard is a cinch to whip up, and it makes a lovely ending to a summer dinner. If blackberries aren't your thing, you can use raspberries or blueberries.

Olive oil, for greasing the baking dish

3 large eggs plus 2 large egg whites

⅓ cup plus 2 tablespoons all-purpose flour

1 teaspoon pure vanilla bean paste or extract

1 teaspoon finely grated lemon zest

1¼ cups heavy cream

3 tablespoons all-purpose flour

Pinch of kosher salt

1 tablespoon minced chives

2 cups fresh blackberries

1 Lightly butter a 9-inch-square glass or ceramic baking dish. In a large bowl, whisk the whole eggs and egg whites with 1/3 cup of the sugar, the vanilla and lemon zest until very stiff, about 1 minute. Whisk in the skim milk, then slowly whisk in the flour and salt until combined. Pour 1 cup of the cake batter into the prepared baking dish and bake for 12 minutes, or until set.

2 Spread the blueberries over the custard and sprinkle with the remaining 2 tablespoons of sugar. Pour the remaining custard on top and bake for about 5 minutes, or until the custard is golden and set in the center. Serve frozen.

Strawberry-Rhubarb Crisp

Serves 8

If you see fresh rhubarb stalks at your market, grab them! This recipe is a breeze to put together and screams seasonality—though in truth, you can buy pretty great frozen rhubarb at most stores now. Do not forget the ice cream here.

1 cup plus 3 tablespoons all-purpose flour

⅔ cup packed dark brown sugar

½ teaspoon kosher salt

1 stick cold unsalted butter, melted

2 pints ripe strawberries, hulled and sliced

1½ rhubarb stalks, cut into ½-inch slices

1 cup sugar

1 teaspoon finely grated orange zest

1 tablespoon fresh orange juice

2 teaspoons pure vanilla extract

Vanilla ice cream, for serving

1 In a medium bowl, combine 1 cup of the flour with the light brown sugar, salt and butter. Using a pastry blender or your fingers, vigorously mix the ingredients together until large crumbs form. Keep the crisp topping refrigerated unless you're using it right away.

2 In a large bowl, toss the whole strawberries and rhubarb slices with the granulated sugar, lemon zest, lemon juice and vanilla until combined. Spoon the fruit into a 9-by-13-inch baking dish. Crumble the topping over the filling. Bake for about 1 hour and 20 minutes, or until the crisp topping is pale and the fruit is bubbling. Let cool slightly before serving the crisp with vanilla ice cream.

LEVEL
HARD

Peach Galette

Makes one (12-inch) galette

Galettes are so adaptable that everyone should have them in their repertoire. If you don't like peaches, you can use nectarines, plums or berries. Apples and pears also make great galettes!

Dough

1¼ cups all-purpose flour, plus more for dusting the work surface and rolling pin

1 tablespoon granulated sugar

½ teaspoon kosher salt

1 stick cold unsalted butter, greated on the large holes of a box grater and frozen

¼ cup ice water mixed with 1 teaspoon red wine vinegar

1 egg mixed with 1 teaspoon water

Coarse sugar, for sprinkling the crust

Filling

3 cups fresh peaches, halved

¼ cup granulated sugar

1 tablespoon cornstarch

1 teaspoon pure vanilla extract

1 teaspoon fresh lemon juice

½ teaspoon kosher salt

1 **Make the cookie dough.** In a food processor, pulse the flour, granulated sugar and salt until combined. Add the frozen butter and pulse until the dough resembles coarse meal. Slowly pulse in the ice water mixture and process just until the dough starts to come together. Turn the dough out onto a work surface and pat into a disk. Wrap in plastic and refrigerate for at least 30 minutes and up to 2 days.

2 **Make the filling.** In a small bowl, toss the sliced peaches with the granulated sugar, vanilla, lemon juice and salt.

3 Line a large baking sheet with parchment paper. On a lightly floured work surface, using a lightly floured rolling pin, roll out the dough to a 12-inch round; carefully transfer the dough to the prepared sheet. Arrange the peaches on the dough in concentric circles, leaving a 2-inch border around the edge. Scrape any filling from the bowl over the peaches. Fold the edge of the dough up and over the filling, overlapping the dough as necessary.

4 Preheat the oven to 400°F. Bake the galette in the center of the oven for about 35 minutes, rotating the baking sheet halfway through baking, until the crust is golden and the filling is bubbling. Let cool before serving.

Apple Crumble Pie

Makes one 9-inch pie

I find apple pie with a crumble topping irresistible, if only for the crunchy bits you can pick off while it's cooling.

Crust

1 cup all-purpose flour, plus more for dusting the work surface and rolling pin

½ teaspoon kosher salt

⅓ cup vegetarian shortening

¼ cup ice water

Filling

7 medium Granny Smith apples—peeled, halved, cored and very thinly sliced

½ cup granulated sugar

3 tablespoons all-purpose flour

2 teaspoons fresh lemon juice

1 teaspoon ground cinnamon

½ teaspoon kosher salt

Topping

¾ cup packed dark brown sugar

¾ cup all-purpose flour

½ teaspoon freshly grated nutmeg

½ teaspoon baking soda

½ teaspoon kosher salt

5 tablespoons unsalted butter, at room temperature

1 **Make the crust.** In a large skillet, pulse the flour and salt with the shortening until coarse crumbs form. Pulse in the ice water, 1 tablespoon at a time, until the dough just starts to come together. Turn the dough out onto a work surface, pat into a disk and wrap in plastic. Refrigerate for at least 30 minutes and up to 2 days.

2 **Make the filling.** In a medium bowl, toss the apples, pears, granulated sugar, flour, lemon juice, cinnamon and salt until warm and combined. Set aside.

3 Preheat the oven to 400°F and position a rack on the lowest shelf. On a floured work surface, using a lightly floured rolling pin, roll out the dough to a 12-inch round. Carefully transfer the dough to a 12-inch pie plate. Trim the excess dough, leaving a 1-inch overhang. Crimp the overhang decoratively.

4 **Make the frosting.** In a medium bowl, stir together the light brown sugar, flour, nutmeg, baking soda and salt. Add the butter and rub the mixture with your fingers until sandy. Press the mixture into clumps and sprinkle over the apple filling.

5 Bake the pie for about 10 minutes, or until the topping is golden brown and the crust is bubbling; cover the edge of the pie if it begins to darken. Let cool on a rack before serving.

LEVEL
HARD

Maple Walnut Pie

Makes one 12-inch pie

If you like both walnuts and pecan pie, then this dessert is for you. It's really simple to make, but for an even easier prep, use store-bought pie crust. The pie goes in the hotter oven before lowering the temperature for baking.

Crust

1¼ cups all-purpose flour, plus more for dusting the work surface and rolling pin

¼ teaspoon kosher salt

1 stick cold unsalted butter, diced

¼ cup hot water

Filling

1½ cups walnuts

3 large eggs

1 cup pure maple syrup

⅓ cup granulated sugar

4 tablespoons unsalted butter, melted

1 teaspoon pure vanilla extract

½ teaspoon kosher salt

Whipped cream, for serving

1 **Make the cake.** In a food processor, pulse the flour and salt with the cold diced butter until coarse crumbs form. Pulse in the ice water, 1 tablespoon at a time, until the dough is thoroughly blended and very well mixed. Turn the dough out onto a work surface, pat into a disk and wrap in plastic. Refrigerate for at least 3 minutes and for up to 2 days.

2 **Make the filling.** Preheat the oven to 200°F and position a rack on the middle shelf. Spread the walnuts on a small rimmed baking sheet or in a pie plate and toast, stirring occasionally, until just nutty-smelling and lightly golden, about 5 minutes. Transfer to a plate to cool.

3 On a floured work surface, using a damp rolling pin, roll out the dough to a 12-inch round. Carefully transfer the dough to a 9-inch pie plate. Trim the excess dough, leaving a 6-inch overhang. Crimp the overhang decoratively.

4 In a large bowl, whisk the eggs with the sugar, melted butter, vanilla and salt. Spread the cooled walnuts in the pie crust and pour the filling over the nuts. Put the pie in the oven and lower the temperature to 350°F. Bake for about 45 minutes, or until the pie is golden. Transfer to a rack and let cool completely before serving. Serve with ice cream.

WORD SEARCHES

You know the drill for these puzzles: Circle each word in the search (they might be horizontal, vertical, diagonal, or backward), and get hungry!
Answers start on page 149.

THE FISH COUNTER

Anchovy	Flounder	Oysters
Barramundi	Lobster	Salmon
Branzino	Mackerel	Shrimp
Clams	Mussels	Swordfish
Crabs	Octopus	Tuna

```
B O N I Z N A R B M X S A S F
O A D S C B S U A G S L N B P
R M R E M H I C X C W E C A Y
N E H R R A K N H X O S H R V
S H D I A E L H Z U R S O C V
Q E M N R M S C B J D U V U L
Y P M E U N U P B B F M Y N R
Q B L L H O O N Z L I C E S B
N O M L A S L C D G S V R O A
L O B S T E R F T I H E E N G
Z W G Q N M X C Z O T C U K Z
S Y A Y J L N S M S P T D H X
P X Y N I E D J Y W R U R V Q
J W U I L A D O D Y J A S Z C
A U M L N X U Y C G T G T R L
```

FOR THE SWEET TOOTH

Blondies
Brownies
Cobbler
Cookies
Cornbread

Cupcakes
Danish
Doughnuts
Eclair
Meringue

Muffins
Pudding
Semifreddo
Shortbread
Tiramisu

```
S B T E Z C E T D Y C X S N S
T S R Q U C O A U U E N J A Y
D O N O L G E B P H I S H D K
Z Z O A W R N C B F M G D A B
Z S I O B N A I F L X N A N L
U R S N D K I U R W E C E I O
C V R P E D M E W E X R R S N
L O Z S G J E I S U M P B H D
C C U S I M A R I T X U T S I
P Q B O B A S C F Z Y J R E E
D O U G H N U T S I F S O I S
T E P U D D I N G K M P H K Z
T X S E Z B T P G Y M E S O R
R B C F Z N C K C H G M S O Q
Z W A Y H I O Z N U A E N C I
```

CHEFS OF THE AGES

Adria
Beard
Blumenthal
Bocuse
Bourdain

Chang
Child
Ducasse
Escoffier
Keller

Morimoto
Pepin
Puck
Redzepi
Robuchon

```
B O O A K J G B L B J E E H V
T L A T X E O N E C M S S F J
B B U J O U L A A N X C S Q L
V O I M R M R L Y H F O A F E
Y O G D E D I A E T C F C J C
G Z A M R N F R Q R A F U B H
N I P E P K T L O E F I D E I
N Z A M C J A H A M N E G I L
K B A U C X I N A B Z R P M D
O Z P M M E R O T L W E N D I
K M W J X O D F A B Z U R J E
B O C U S E A H W D C L Q T V
E V F Q P I R P E Q I I Y E L
E A G L S Z X R J R G X W X U
N O H C U B O R A S U X J T T
```

SAY CHEESE!

Asiago
Brie
Camembert
Cheddar
Gorgonzola

Gouda
Gruyere
Havarti
Manchego
Mascarpone

Mozzarella
Parmigiano
Pecorino
Provolone
Ricotta

```
A L M P V W P V J G U O L Y N
G L O A D K K A O M S N Q U W
I O L E N O P R A C S A M K X
L T G E G C G B T E C I P J E
V M R A R O H R R H S G E P J
O N I A N A E E E I A I C W B
J S T Z V B Z D G V E M O A Z
A R O M M A D Z E O P R R T D
L L K E P A H A O H O A I T L
A B M S R C U J B M K P N O V
I A P R O V O L O N E A O C E
C B R G W Z U K C L H N K I Y
E R E Y U R G V I A E F F R K
B G O U D A S E F X S Z P P K
V N L Y B Q B T D A G E Z P U
```

BREAD, BREAD, BREAD

Baguette
Barbari
Biscuit
Brioche
Challah

Chapati
Ciabatta
Focaccia
Lavash
Naan

Paratha
Pita
Pumpernickel
Sourdough
Tortilla

```
P I T A H D E Z N G R P H C A
N A J K C Z V T I S U I P H T
T A C K J K D J T M M Z P A T
I H A W T C V M P E I E P L A
U R S N J F M E N K U A V L B
C H G U O D R U O S I G C A A
S Q N R Q N B L I C G H A H I
I W X K I I Y R C R A Y S B C
B O K C L P J A I P A A V U X
V M K A Z U C Q A O V B V A M
I E S X L O U T K A C S R O I
L Q P G F H I A L B G H F A I
D L O U T O R T I L L A E G B
S I C X M C Z Z A H T A R A P
E H S C E S L D T I W G L G G
```

IN THE KITCHEN

Blender
Casserole
Colander
Dishwasher
Knife

Ladle
Microplane
Oven
Processor
Refrigerator

Saucepan
Skillet
Spatula
Spoon
Toaster

```
F I B T C I T L K H F S L E D
N R Y G Z A A E I N A O N P H
I O A Q Z D S X L U I A X R J
Q T G Y L I Y S C L L F M O J
C A V E H O S E E P I L E C G
L R W S I U P Q O R R K P E O
W E H F E A P R M E O S S S W
A G P R N T C D D S R L W S I
L I Q S S I K N Y I M J E O G
U R S Y M R E D N A L O C R A
T F P S T L T O A S T E R N R
A E O C B S G S P Y W N E V O
P R O U P D I S H W A S H E R
S G N E G C J E L L Z Y Q H F
B G B G A H H V S D I F K Q H
```

THE BAKER'S PANTRY

Baking Soda   Cornstarch   Salt
Butter   Cream   Shortening
Chocolate   Eggs   Sugar
Cinnamon   Flour   Vanilla
Cocoa   Molasses   Yeast

```
S Y O B E T A L O C O H C X S
O H Z M A K B F X D N A Z H G
O H D X P K L X M V L L O S G
Y Z R C H O I S K L M R A M E
O S J O U C T N I M T K Y S S
S K Y R N L O N G E T N F F E
C H E N A O A C N S A B M I S
I S Z S U V M I O K O K M Y S
B U T T E R N A T A I D X C A
I G X A X G O H N S V H A R L
C V C R G H I O E N A S R E O
Y C D C C V E V J E I E Q A M
A I Z H S U K Z C W W C Y M Z
K C R E R A G U S E X E V S B
V C Q N Y E H B C U R L K R O
```

IT'S FIVE O'CLOCK SOMEWHERE

Boulevardier
Caipirinha
Cosmopolitan
Daiquiri
Gimlet

Manhattan
Margarita
Martini
Mimosa
Mojito

Negroni
Paloma
Sazerac
Screwdriver
Sidecar

```
T K B S A P D I U C B S I A B
K E I O A T N P A F X A R S X
B T L L U I I T K P Z I O D
Y H O M T L P R C L S E U M Y
J M D R I I E N A K T R Q I S
A K A Y R G J V E G B A I M C
C M F I B V U L A G R C A O R
Z R N S I D E C A R R A D A E
I H O T I J O M M Y D O M E W
A D K K K E K F U R F I N E D
C O S M O P O L I T A N E I R
X N A T T A H N A M K R W R I
W W U H J G F S M B R T E T V
F P P S Y U B L T W T Y S N E
J Q E W H B S E S D S N D W R
```

WHAT'S YOUR PASTA?

Bucatini
Campanelle
Cavatappi
Ditalini
Fusilli

Gemelle
Linguine
Malfadine
Orecchiette
Orzo

Pappardelle
Penne
Rigatoni
Spaghetti
Tagliatelle

```
E N N E P U W Q C B T G F E S
E N I D A F L A M O F W U N P
K Y V A I H V I E S R E S I A
L W L L W A N Y T L L T I U G
W G C Z T I I G T L F R L G H
P T Q A L M E N E A E W L N E
U S P A M M T D I O J R I I T
T P T R E P R Q H T Z X P L T
I I W L C A A Q C E A R X A I
D Y L Z P N I N C D Q C O F K
O E N P F S U R E P G P U F N
K S A L B Y N Y R L D M A B F
I P A D A S R F O X L B X V R
T A G L I A T E L L E E E Q T
R I G A T O N I P P D G K H O
```

FROM THE APPLE ORCHARD

Braeburn
Cameo
Cortland
Empire
Fuji

Gala
Granny Smith
Honey Crisp
Jonagold
Macoun

McIntosh
Mutsu
Pink Lady
Red Delicious
Rome

```
O  G  U  M  P  O  X  F  Q  D  X  R  P  L  D
Q  E  A  P  V  B  H  H  L  V  E  Q  I  G  S
A  H  M  L  S  A  K  O  M  D  E  I  N  P  Z
U  S  E  A  A  I  G  B  D  W  M  U  K  T  M
Q  O  M  U  C  A  R  E  R  A  H  Z  L  S  O
T  T  F  K  N  Y  L  C  C  A  V  Q  A  F  G
U  N  S  O  U  I  N  O  Y  D  E  T  D  R  F
S  I  J  N  C  F  U  J  I  E  Q  B  Y  G  A
T  C  R  I  T  N  L  B  V  V  D  U  P  R
U  M  O  E  R  I  P  M  E  V  K  O  C  R  Q
M  U  E  H  I  S  X  M  K  B  E  P  H  H
S  U  E  C  K  S  O  T  R  A  Z  Y  M  V  G
I  B  D  L  R  R  K  D  T  Z  X  N  Z  O  Z
H  H  T  I  M  S  Y  N  N  A  R  G  W  M  N
V  B  M  C  O  R  T  L  A  N  D  U  H  B  S
```

MEET YOUR MEAT

Brisket
Chuck Roast
Flank
Flat Iron
Ground Beef

Hanger
New York Strip
Porterhouse
Ribeye
Rib Roast

Short Rib
Sirloin
Skirt
Tenderloin
Tri Tip

```
P E T S A O R B I R F C T T E
C S S T K T P Q L L D M S E T
D S G U Q N F S A M O R A N E
Y C D C O Q R N O J L R O D K
T N W R X H K W R Z F N R E S
P I R T S K R O Y W E N K R I
G R O U N D B E E F F B C L R
H A N G E R B N T L C D U O B
D R P V L Z I I A R Y F H I T
B E I K Z O G T R Y O H C N R
G V G B L L I O R T O P F O I
A T C R E R U A Z T R I K S T
Z O I N O Y H C I A O O D E I
D S S N N R E W F H Z N H S P
R F Q A P X K K T Y Z U L S P
```

THE SPICE RACK

Allspice
Caraway
Cardamom
Chili Powder
Cinnamon

Cloves
Coriander
Cumin
Fennel
Five Spice

Nutmeg
Paprika
Saffron
Star Anise
Turmeric

```
C A C H R N D M V C P R R Z J
F I J L U E N R A Q E U E S I
I A R T O B J R C D E A D F M
R U M E S V D M N H K L W E N
S E D N M A E A K I N I O N E
G T V Q M R I S R L V B P N P
A Y A O Y R U P S U L I I E P
L A M R O B A T E S Y R L L K
L W A C A P F I V E S P I C E
S A N X L N I M U C X V H G W
P R T J Q T I X Q Y V F C Q K
I A G U P R E S A F F R O N A
C C Y W H W J B E L H M V B C
E K D D N O M A N N I C Z R Q
A T P T E S O S I R T B Q V F
```

SALAD BAR 101

Bacon Bits
Beans
Beets
Broccoli
Carrot

Celery
Cheese
Chickpeas
Croutons
Cucumber

Lettuce
Nuts
Onion
Pepper
Tomato

```
L D S C W U E B C C J S Y R K
A W S K E C Y H F H J X G E X
U K U N U L I L P E Q Q I B P
S I K T O C E E I E B O P M D
Y N T W K T P R T S A D Z U S
J E A P W P U I Y E C K K C U
L M E E E I L O C C O R B U G
H A B R B I S I R K N T H C F
S O T A M O T S G C B R V X Y
C A R R O T E D X I I X S J T
I P G T R T E N Y N T J N L Y
D R E B D B B K U F S O I I X
K K N U T S D N N B I H V R B
L J E I K J U U J N U A Z L S
T G N G G Z D F O C G V P V S
```

SUSHI, PLEASE

Ahi
Hamachi
Hirame
Hotate
Ikura

Kanpachi
Made
Maguro
Mentaiko
Saba

Sake
Sawara
Tobiko
Toro
Unagi

```
Y P K Z V Q H I J A G V J F Y
M N S K H H H A S K R S Z H T
B S F V O C Q Q M Y Q A Q I N
V P E T A E H D B A G B W R H
V Z A P M O R O T Q C A V A L
X T N O N A E M T J S H X M S
E A V K E C D W R A V Y I E H
K V Q I C J B E K N A I F W
I U O B M V P E G R X F H V T
M T T O S P O Z U F Q X X A Z
D L M T T G Y K U N A G I N G
N G R A S E I M E N T A I K O
H W E F G E C Y T W L Y A I Q
D P P Z V J A B S O R U G A M
K Y K O N T L I W C S S L M J
```

UMAMI BOMBS

Anchovies
Bottarga
Ketchup
Kimchi
Miso

Mushrooms
Olives
Parmesan
Prosciutto
Sauerkraut

Soy Sauce
Tomatoes
Truffles
Vinegar
Worcestershire

```
B L O I T D F T N P P O Q B P
Y O V L O L R Y R A U T S N W
T S T H I U J A W R H T H Z B
R U V T F V G Z S M C U L O C
E N A F A E E E B E T I D G T
X C L R N R I S N S E C U M P
V E U I K V G Z U A K S F G R
S T V A O R W A Y N Y O I H J
E R I H S R E T S E C R O W M
A D C V C Y W U T L D P O Y I
E N X M S E O T A M O T R R S
A K I M C H I S S S H T C S O
W R W D U N M Y M J P W V E P
V W B D A Z R P Q J G E L O T
M U S H R O O M S G P L T X A
```

TV CHEFS

Brown
Cora
De Laurentiis
Fieri
Flay

Garten
Goldman
Lagasse
Lawson
Ramsay

Ray
Symon
Tosi
Tsai
Yan

```
N  S  I  I  T  N  E  R  U  A  L  E  D  F  B
R  A  N  O  M  Y  S  E  L  A  W  S  O  N  R
R  A  M  A  O  L  L  S  E  Y  T  B  F  Y  O
O  A  M  D  R  L  I  S  I  A  B  I  N  A  W
K  P  Y  S  L  O  K  A  I  N  E  E  G  L  N
D  Q  E  K  A  O  C  G  F  R  T  L  B  F  T
F  L  E  N  X  Y  G  A  I  R  I  Q  E  D  G
B  Q  N  Y  T  N  J  L  A  S  B  O  X  C  W
S  Z  M  A  H  K  G  G  O  A  Y  T  D  Q  H
I  Y  B  X  C  E  X  T  A  B  M  O  L  R  A
Z  O  S  C  J  P  E  G  N  I  P  K  D  V  Q
F  J  M  S  X  W  O  C  E  U  M  F  L  J  W
B  F  I  M  B  W  W  S  Z  M  X  Z  I  H  I
R  T  V  R  E  W  U  A  G  F  T  S  A  I  C
G  P  Q  W  E  P  R  Y  K  M  K  U  E  R  K
```

SO, HOW IS IT?

Bitter
Bland
Cheesy
Creamy
Crispy

Crunchy
Doughy
Flaky
Gooey
Lemony

Nutty
Peppery
Pickled
Salty
Spicy

```
A G Q N Y N Y C Q E E A Y Z D
C Q H C Q G H H Y E O O G E Y
Z D I X F X C E B B D O L B N
H P Z N T T N E E G C K C Q O
S F S I F S U S N R C C U V M
B P E P P E R Y I I F Y S H E
S I O O N Z C S P Y J L O S L
A B T U X I P S J H H H A V J
L M T T I Y B L A N D G X K W
T T C P E Z A O P H P T U I Y
Y I F A U R O Y X X V J W O K
P R N C X X Q K Y U G G U M D
V V G T B B E N M A V F S T Q
W Q H D G E X D W N F F F R L
Y M A E R C L T L I W W O X L
```

COFFEE FOR ALL

Affogato	Dark Roast	Mocha
Americano	Espresso	Nitro Brew
Barista	Flat White	Pour Over
Cappuccino	Latte	Redeye
Cold Drip	Macchiato	Ristretto

```
B F O L F K F A R O E A P W R
E T I S N L F X T X T A Z R E
I U S E S F A A F A I L A I V
B F X A O E I T T Q H H N S O
F K M G O H R S T C W Z D T R
U W A I C R I P A E T X L R U
L T D C A R K P S Q A F Z E O
O A A D A R P R C E L S H T P
N M T B L U K U A M F X F T M
A E V T C P I R D D L O C O O
W N J C O N A C I R E M A M C
T U I E R E D E Y E P Y Q L H
P N W M I A N U O S I A L A A
O N I T R O B R E W B F U I G
O N C M Q E R J F V V O B J F
```

EAT YOUR VEGGIES

Artichokes
Asparagus
Bok Choy
Broccoli
Cabbage

Carrots
Cauliflower
Celery
Eggplant
Fennel

Kale
Leeks
Mushrooms
Spinach
Turnips

```
R P M Z E I S N F Y C A S D N
L E T T G K E B M E O F P O S
E T W U G U K O R O N F C U Z
E I D O P B O S N O R G F S
K R B Z L V H K T M C A E P G
S O T F A F C C F O R C I L O
S Y A M N H I O C A R N O J H
Z F K F T F T L P P R R B L D
C E L E R Y R S U U N O A H I
V E G A B B A C T A K G K C X
M U S H R O O M S C C A J A H
J K O S B R E A H F L E T N A
X G O C P P G O W E B L N I E
D J L M D X Y M H B F M X P P
T Z N T O V J I S Z I F U S R
```

WINE GRAPES

Albarino
Barbera
Chardonnay
Chenin Blanc
Gamay

Malbec
Merlot
Pinot Noir
Riesling
Sangiovese

Syrah
Tempranillo
Vermentino
Viognier
Zinfandel

```
W E R Q G A K W S O T H W V O
D C A U E E J H D E G V F V N
M K J C W S R I M Z I A B C I
G Y M C R G E P X O C J U Q T
Z U R H O N R V G W N J Y M N
H V I E Y A N N O D R A H C E
X P E N N A I W S I M U R M M
V E S I Q E L O Z A G I R O R
U R L N R Y B G C O N I E E E
T L I B A G B F A N E L A K V
O P N L X V C D T R R B Q S O
L H G A S D N O I M I T L H I
R Z I N F A N D E L O N M A M
E B T C S I S Y R A H J O U M
M L G E P A R E B R A B J B P
```

IT'S THE RICE

Bibimbap	Katsudon	Pilaf
Biryani	Kedgeree	Risotto
Congee	Nasi Goreng	Suman
Jambalaya	Onigiri	Sushi
Jollof Rice	Paella	Tahdig

```
P Q Q Y S X Q B K T K C T P E
T W O U E S L A A G E O J O U
Q U M T U B T E N D D N Y D L
J A E Q T S W E D S G G I F U
N A X B U O R S E I E E N I I
C L M D Q O S I U Z R E A H V
C T O B G H R I V D E R Y K D
F N A I A I L M R Z E Q R J Q
G A S H G L P A B M I B I B A
C A L I D P A E L L A D B T U
N A N I V I K Y I H S U S S W
N O Z L P Y G L A B E H C I Y
O A M V E Q S G T N M Y Y G I
H M J J O L L O F R I C E C W
I M G I G T N O Q Q W U M V N
```

AH, THE AROMA

Basil
Bergamot
Cardamom
Chocolate
Cinnamon

Cloves
Cumin
Coffee
Ginger
Jasmine

Lavender
Lemongrass
Mint
Oregano
Rosemary

```
R A T D L T P E D O X V B M J
L O J O L A V E N D E R L O A
A R S D M W Y O V O F E M M S
Y U T E U A M R R W M B N A M
M Q T Z M A G E D O Y S Z D I
Z I B L N A G R N V O E R R N
L Y N N R A R G E T Y O R A E
L E I T N Z R Y H B E E I C R
B C E O M A S E V O L C Q L V
K R G F S Y L P M T C M R A U
G M A S F I Z C T B N U E C W
Z Z X V S O W F D W S D G H X
O Y Y A W F C C U M I N N Q G
B J B I W P E B R H T O I O O
E T A L O C O H C I N Q G V L
```

TIME FOR BREAKFAST

Bacon
Bagels
Cereal
Eggs
French Toast

Granola
Hash Browns
Muesli
Muffins
Oatmeal

Omelet
Pancakes
Sausage
Scones
Waffles

```
H B A R O K B W L A E M T A O
F A E E Y Y A B P Y U O L W A
V G S M S F R B Q E O W H S B
N E H H F C D A S I T G O F V
B L C L B A O L T P X M R M L
I S E P T R I N C N B A I Q S
E S G O T Y O G E C X N K H N
Y R F L S A V W O S E C K E I
C E R E A L L R N G P A O X F
F R E N C H T O A S T K Z P F
T E L E M O K S N N L E R S U
V W M G F N U J E A O S T G M
I A M N D A Q X U E R C G G W
J Z F E S K K S N A Y G A E D
M S I A W N J W Y V Y P I B F
```

PEPPERS, HOT AND SWEET

Anaheim   Fresno   Pimento
Banana   Guajillo   Piquillo
Bell   Habanero   Poblano
Cayenne   Jalapeño   Serrano
Cubanelle   Pasilla   Shishito

```
E C B A B F Y C Y T C P N A O
N N U C N H K N T Q L E P N Q
O Q N B Z A O Y P O R I S B U
H L Y E A D H Z A K Q E A U K
F W L C Y N P E S U R M N V O
G F Q I S A E V I F C J A T N
P N I L J U C L L M F L N R S
A O Q L S A L J L K T E A L N
O R O J H O U B A E M N B H Q
I E R D I P C G J I B E L L G
X N L Y S X W A P O B L A N O
A A T O H O N E P A L A J P S
P B Q X I N O N A R R E S E V
M A H L T O D I U N H V V D U
S H D L O B L Q C D J Q X J A
```

SPEAKING FRENCH

Bisque
Bouillabaisse
Cassoulet
Choucroute
Coq au Vin

Crêpes
Eclair
Gougère
Niçoise
Quiche

Ratatouille
Rillettes
Soufflé
Tarte Tatin
Velouté

```
O Q L E G T Y B P M E R R K E
J C K S U R A E I L N I N L S
M V P S J Y P R F S L W L C I
F Q A I J M E F T L Q I S R O
P P J A S C U S E E U U B E C
T L C B L O E T N O T A E P I
C C G A S C T R T G O A L E N
A X I L V E F A E S R Y T S S
S R D L S Z T Q D G N G B I K
S C L I W A V E L O U T E Y N
O T V U R C H O U C R O U T E
U X N O N I V U A Q O C G G X
L E K B V E H C I U Q T B T B
E M U G Y A A B B E A W M V R
T H G N Z Q R C V P P X U P Z
```

CROSSWORDS

Each of these crosswords includes some themed clues
(look to the puzzle title for a hint). Answers start on page 156.

1 "Life is just ____ of ..."
6 Domesticate
10 Drink that is good with 36-Across
14 Hawaiian patio
15 Human rights lawyer Clooney
16 Opera solo
17 Weasel out of
18 Pause
19 Snoopy
20 Sweet biscuit made with a rolled grain and dried grapes
23 The Opry channel, once
24 "We Wish ____ Merry ..."
25 Sweet biscuit made with refined grain and refined cacao
31 Spy org.
33 Neighborhood grp.
34 Despots
35 Tolkien monster
36 Subjects of this puzzle
39 Auntie, in Aragon
40 Proportion
42 Immigrant's class: Abbr.
43 Superlative suffix
44 Sweet biscuit made with refined sugar and cookie cutters
49 "I ____ Spicy Pepper"
50 Tavern
51 Sweet biscuit made by rolling the dough in a sugar-cinnamon combo
57 Sweet biscuit made into a tiny sandwich
59 Helper
60 Unleash
61 Brooklet
62 Retired Senate Majority Leader Harry
63 "Do ____ myself clear?"
64 Top medal
65 Sp. miss
66 Shoe parts

1 Too
2 Island band The ____ Men
3 "Step ____ "
4 Gentle heat
5 ____ other (unparalleled)
6 Stately
7 Type of leopard or tiger from the Russian-Chinese border
8 Southeast Asian peninsula
9 Filmdom's Billy who loved to dance
10 Musical group 10,000 ____
11 Ore you can pump
12 Fleur de ____
13 Jay follower
21 Mole sauce chile
22 Tallow sources
25 Prickly desert dwellers
26 Winner at tic-tac-toe
27 L.A. pro player
28 Intolerant one
29 Flag flower
30 Standardized test for sophs.
31 Mrs. Dithers
32 Iraq's neighbor
36 Tropical raccoon relative
37 "This ____ test"
38 Spanish hero
41 "____ Cowhand" (Bing Crosby song)
45 Bygone Renaults
46 Using an extra egg white might make a sweet biscuit this
47 "All I ____ what you tell me"
48 Humongous, informally
51 Vend
52 Fix text
53 The scarlet letter
54 *Let's Make a ____*
55 Erie, for one
56 ____ out a living (makes ends meet)
57 URL ending
58 Kia model

BISCUITS

ACROSS

1 Pack _____ (prepare for a trip)
5 Con
9 Understood
14 Zilch
15 "Where _____?"
16 *Life on Mars* star Jason
17 Pomegranate seed
18 Camaro _____ - Z (classic '80s model)
19 Early spring bloom
20 "Why Must _____ Teenager" (Red Hot Chili Peppers song)
21 Acerbic
22 Shoelace tip
23 Bloom on a pumpkin relative
26 Fruity dessert tart
27 Slew
28 "Able was I _____ I saw Elba"
31 Bloom named for a legendary beast
36 White winter coat?
37 Bird of prey
38 Nibble from a pod
39 Strike _____ (get ready for a photo)
40 Exhaust
41 Bachelor's button bloom or shade of blue
43 Pub order
44 *2001* computer
45 Lawyer: Abbr.
46 Blooms that are the subject of this puzzle
53 Frosts
55 Ear-related
56 Give off
57 *Me, Myself &* _____ (Jim Carrey film)
58 Words of woe
59 Stow cargo
60 Johnny-jump-up bloom, e.g.
61 Indian bread
62 "I _____ pony" (Beatles lyric)
63 Lauder of cosmetics
64 Photo blowups: Abbr.
65 Snow slider

DOWN

1 Nin who wrote *Delta of Venus*
2 Cookout, for short
3 French farewell
4 Crunchy pome variety from New Zealand
5 Basketball shot
6 Chocolate imitation
7 "Don't tell _____ !"
8 Bit of funding for a small business
9 Built _____ (sturdy)
10 Friend, in Madrid
11 "_____ for your free reading!" (psychic Miss Cleo's tagline)
12 "Dies _____" (ancient hymn)
13 Social grace
24 *West _____ Story*
25 Family member
29 Valentine bloom
30 Pitcher
31 *Go _____ Watchman* (Harper Lee novel)
32 Claw
33 Accord
34 Tragic lunar mission of 1967
35 Neighbor of Pol.
36 Fuses with metal in small areas
39 Choir member
41 Taxi
42 Atlanta pro team
44 "_____ Is on the Sparrow" (gospel tune popularized by Whitney Houston)
47 Thick
48 Patriot Allen
49 Kind of exam
50 Online missive
51 Blue _____ Mountains
52 Lieu
53 Ready to eat
54 Nest-egg letters

BLOOM

1 Bad grades
5 Jane Austen novel
9 "Peace on earth, good will _____"
14 Knot or singer Ives
15 Meadows
16 Justice Samuel
17 Subject of this crossword
19 Home of Moscow and Boise
20 Barley bristle
21 Paddle
23 Max's opposite
24 Request
26 Citrus drink
31 Place for an icon
33 Former spouses
34 Soothing salve
35 Spirit
37 "_____ Haw!"
39 Colorful and sweet morning pastry
45 "Cigar City," Florida, airport abbr.
46 Pro vote
47 Ships driven by ETs
48 Way back when
51 Triangle with unequal sides
53 Food made with bread soaked in an egg wash
57 Sine's reciprocal, in trig: Abbr.
58 Poetic contraction
59 Rm. coolers
60 Sup, as 17-Across
62 Morning kick?
65 Diner potatoes
70 Notions
71 Spirit
72 Former Chevy model
73 Topping for 53-Across
74 Act
75 Alternative to suspenders

1 Recede
2 Animal's coat
3 Comes unglued
4 Cole_____
5 Tolkien creature
6 "Oh, give _____ home where the buffalo roam . . . "
7 Stone worker
8 "All the world's _____"
9 Mai _____
10 Ancient
11 Dolphins' home
12 Moral
13 Nary a soul
18 Tangle
22 Tyrannosaurus _____
24 Small amount of gel
25 Vend
27 What you'd use to make 18-Down
28 Mimic
29 Drive like _____
30 Handy
32 Persist
36 Snoop
38 Competent
40 French court
41 "Daniel Boone was a man, _____ big man"
42 Apple computers
43 Charged particles
44 Tiny amt. of time
49 "_____ -ching!"
50 Engraved
52 Crown of Osiris
53 Cat genus
54 Prepared
55 PC key on the right of the keyboard
56 "_____ mio"
61 Bedouin or his steed
63 Letter after sigma
64 Sixth sense
66 _____ West
67 Stop
68 Skinny fish
69 Drunk

BRUNCH

ACROSS

1 A cold one
5 Pie with pepperoni
10 Base for Asian cuisine
14 Wine: Prefix
15 Throw _____ in the fountain
16 Walker on Hoth
17 Part of a seat
18 Babbled
19 Quick office note
20 Univ. or Inst.
21 She launched a thousand ships
22 Melon anagram
23 Try to pick up
25 Charged particle
26 What you might heat up in 44-Across
30 Opponent
33 Something you might get at a pool
34 Top of a church or tower
35 Say grace
36 Green stone
37 Airport screening grp.
38 Memorized
39 "I smell _____"
40 Comedians
42 Bottle amts.
43 Fuel
44 See 26-Across and 30-Down
46 Uncle_____ (patriotic figure)
47 Literary surprise
49 Alluring aroma
52 Source of phones and pies
55 Christmas tree type
57 Mama's mate
58 Take a base without a hit
59 Writer of verses
60 _____the Red
61 _____of Two Cities
62 Part in a play
63 Ship's flooring
64 Out of fashion
65 Chances

DOWN

1 Tries for apples in autumn
2 Stretch for
3 Rolled tortillas with sauce
4 Stir-fry pan
5 Call them when you're broke
6 Planner on your iPhone
7 Daydream during class, with "out"
8 Utah National Park with red peaks
9 _____ Arbor (University of Michigan home)
10 Mainstay of a college diet
11 Thing
12 Blend-in color
13 School of royals
21 Rock and Roll's is in Cleveland, Ohio
22 _____ Alamos, New Mexico
24 Doctrine
25 Anger
27 Eye-related
28 Protector for the eyes
29 Muse of poetry
30 What you might heat up in 44-Across
31 Snacks for horses
32 A thing powered by 27-Down's nerve
33 Plantation in *Gone with the Wind*
35 City in Utah
36 British car, for short
40 Edge of a crater
41 Drank a 1-Across
44 Yoga class essential
45 "_____ we there yet?"
46 Popcorn is a popular one
48 Triangular street sign
49 Exceeded the limit
50 Show concern
51 _____ of Gilgamesh (ancient story)
52 Lead-in to boy or girl
53 Flavor in whiskey
54 A _____ horse (Death's steed)
56 Hwys.
58 Dejected
59 Vet

COLLEGE FOOD

ACROSS

1 Miners' sch.
5 Ziti, for example
10 Circuit
14 French Sudan, today
15 _____ life
16 About, atop a memo: Abbr.
17 Colo. neighbor
18 Wiped out
19 Breaks
20 Cheese in Caprese
22 Pluck
23 Writer Asimov
24 Glimpse
25 Spirit
26 Alien-seeking org.
28 Surrealist Salvador
30 H in Greek
33 _____ in India
35 Mushrooms, in Milan
39 Dish with breaded poultry, tomato sauce and cheese
43 Sweet cold dessert in Bologna
44 Love, in Lucca
45 Doctors' org.
46 Dunham or Horne
48 Immediately
51 Actress Katey of *Sons of Anarchy*
54 Knight's address
56 Locker room poster, maybe
60 Thing
61 Hearty soup of Rome
63 Singer James of jazz
64 Moisten in a recipe
65 Rice-like 5-Across
66 Hair-removal brand
67 Marble type
68 Increase
69 Intro drawing class
70 City of sin in the Bible
71 AOL, MSN, etc.

DOWN

1 Savory taste quality
2 Edible roots
3 Miss Doolittle of *My Fair Lady*
4 Pies of Pisa
5 Jack of a late-night talk show
6 _____ well
7 Archaeological carved stone pillar
8 Shadowed
9 *The Thin Man* dog
10 Flat type of 5-Across
11 Corkers
12 Go around
13 Green sauce for 5-Across
21 Perfect serve
25 Blue
27 Attach with rope
29 Big dos
30 ER test
31 Alexander _____ Great
32 Be unwell
34 Relaxing resort
36 Troop grp.
37 Easter entrée
38 "All _____ day's work"
40 Squid at the *ristorante*
41 Mail-order record co.
42 Almond-flavored liqueur
47 Topping for 5-Across
49 Appropriate
50 Potato-filled relative of 5-Across
51 Tuscan city where you might eat 5-Across
52 Perfume ingredient
53 "Come and _____ !"
55 _____ shape (pathetic)
57 Dunn and Ephron
58 Open, as a duffel bag
59 Drudges
61 Bus. degrees
62 Appear

ITALIAN

1 Ring-shaped roll
6 Three-ingredient sandwich
9 Goes with 37-Across
14 Old Oldsmobile model
15 Summer zodiac sign
16 Handy
17 Lion sounds
18 Phony
20 Hoagie made with meat from a can
22 French pronoun
23 Bank statement abbr.
24 Orb: Abbr.
27 Mineral in bananas
32 Throat dangler
34 Augment: Abbr.
35 Blow up: Abbr.
36 Cowardly
37 Goes with 9-Across
41 Some locker room decorations
42 Dorm VIPs
43 Cuba Libre ingredient
44 Decree
45 When you'd eat 1-, 6-, 9, 20-, 37- or 52-Across
48 Took off
49 Poem of praise
51 Ditty
52 Meal with mayo and poultry
58 Pregnancy division
61 Napped leather
62 Helicopter feature
63 Covert ____
64 Computer message
65 Insipid
66 Hwy.
67 *Inferno* author

1 *Simpsons* boy
2 Moisés or Matty of baseball
3 Heart cherry
4 List of mistakes
5 Defeats
6 Thin Russian pancake
7 What libraries do
8 "...jump off the deep end and learn ____"
9 Critical point
10 Engrave
11 Deception
12 Area with small fallout: Abbr.
13 "____ -haw!"
19 "There's no ____ team"
21 Parts of an estate
24 Mena of *American Beauty*
25 Fully attended assembly
26 ____-downs (outgrown clothes)
27 Habanero or chile
28 Iroquois group
29 *Better Out* ____ (Banksy art residency)
30 Bach's Mass ____ Minor
31 Aboriginal name for Ayers Rock
33 Irreg.
36 MRI alternative
38 Mini PC and game system by Intel
39 Where you might've had it
40 Catch some rays
45 Church reader
46 Warned like a cat
47 Emotional shock
50 Insult
52 "Let's go!"
53 Possessed
54 Once
55 Slender
56 Mine entrance
57 Cut
58 Prefix with angle or cycle
59 Friend of Harry and Hermione
60 Call ____ day)

LUNCH

1   Small talk
5   Reclines
9   Castle water hazards
14 Rice-A-_____
15 "Do _____ others . . ."
16 Burnt _____ (crayon color)
17 First name of Henry VIII's second wife
18 Sign-off from Mork
19 Neptune has 14 of these
20 Part 1 of a quote by George Tillman Jr.
23 Rugby score
24 "Able was I _____ I saw Elba"
25 _____ Angelico
26 Passports, e.g.
29 Part 3 of the quote
32 Oregon's capital
36 Negative responses
37 Prefix with type
38 Prize
39 Three times daily on an Rx
40 Wooden block stacking game
41 Actress O'Grady of *Eight Is Enough*
42 "Eureka!"
43 "_____ my case"
44 Part 4 of the quote
48 East Germany: Abbr.
49 Sault _____ Marie
50 UFO aliens
51 _____ double take
54 Part 2 of the quote
58 Film
60 _____ facto
61 Diabolical
62 Archaeological pillar
63 Hide-and- _____
64 Prima donna
65 Small piece
66 Zeus's wife
67 A whole lot

1   Word after air or witch
2   Venerate
3   Irk
4   7–7, in a way
5   Of the moon
6   Very shortly
7   Volcano on Sicily
8   Deep South cuisine
9   Most populous city in India
10 Melville novel
11 Australian native
12 Nadia Comaneci was the first to get this score, in the 1976 Olympics
13 Year after jrs.
21 Online source for health info
22 Vessels for duos?
27 Minor dents
28 Weasel relative
30 Vegetable that might draw a tear?
31 N.Y. Met, for one
32 Caesar or Waldorf
33 Wave _____ (cast a spell)
34 British Jeep
35 Lake shared by Pennsylvania and Ohio
39 Dishonest
40 Jiu- _____
42 _____ von Bismarck
45 In dreamland
46 Yellowstone feature
47 "_____ lick of my peppermint stick"
51 One who is 61-Across
52 Martini garnish
53 Attorney- _____
55 Nike competitor
56 Thin sword for competition
57 Government agents, for short
58 Authors' submissions: Abbr.
59 One way drugs are sold, for short

QUOTE

1 Verse
5 Bumbling
10 Level
14 Anger
15 *The Terminator* heroine Connor
16 Ounce, in Spain
17 Grps.
18 "There is ____ in the affairs of men": Brutus
19 Disfigure
20 Spicy stew with beans and meat
23 Cookie-selling grp.
25 Progressive Insurance spokeswoman
26 Attendants for royalty
27 Rebellion
30 Pooh's young friend
31 ____ Grosso, Brazil
32 Set ____ of exchange
34 Timetable abbr.
37 Comfort soup with a green cruciferous veggie and cheese
41 Wine: Prefix
42 Early ____
43 Puerto Rico, *por ejemplo*
44 Popular ISP
45 Deli or trattoria
48 "C'est magnifique!"
52 Org. with strikes
53 Opposite of WSW
54 Nutritious soup for the sick
57 ____-nine-tails
58 Iguana genus (anagram of A LION)
59 Therefore, in Latin
62 "I smell ____ !"
63 Round before finals
64 Bring in
65 Marshal Dillon
66 Be
67 Tangle

1 In favor of
2 Scull
3 Container for breakfast makings
4 Come together
5 "Loving You ____ Know" (Pretenders song)
6 Washington team
7 Rocker Clapton
8 ____ paper (a place for notes)
9 Civil War winning side
10 Soup made from a vine fruit
11 Walking arm ____
12 Online mag
13 Japanese noodle soup
21 No ____ , ands or buts
22 Australian bird or Outback call
23 Spicy Cajun soup with okra
24 People in 52-Across might pick this up
28 Summer Games grp.
29 Sorrow
33 Athens tourist attraction
34 Grammy-winning English singer of "Shape of You" and "Thinking Out Loud"
35 Eagle's claw
36 Curtain
38 Toad's call
39 License to drill
40 Insult, slangily
44 Writer Louisa May
46 Woodwind player
47 Pop
48 Reasoner with a "razor"
49 Scarlett of Tara
50 Try to swat
51 Building addition
55 *All the Presidents' Bankers* author Prins
56 Soup made from an onion kin
60 Miracle- ____
61 Canadian prov.

SOUP

1 "Game, _____ , match!"
4 "It's _____ dunk" (sure thing)
9 " _____, I'm Adam" (a famous palindrome)
14 Evil laugh
15 "I _____ vacation!"
16 Awake and ready
17 Bullfight cheer
18 Killed
19 Gets out of bed
20 Chocolatey treat sometimes colored with beet juice
23 Counselor Deanna from *Star Trek: The Next Generation*
24 Money in Spain or Germany
25 Therefore, in logic
28 Los _____ Unidos
31 "I _____ Rock," (Simon & Garfunkel song)
33 The metal with the fewest number of letters
34 Drink after sledding
36 Fudd and Gantry
38 Cold treat with eggs whisked into warm milk, sugar and cornstarch
41 Disputed Black Sea peninsula
42 Large button on the right of a keyboard
43 Grp. in charge of Summer Games
44 Code responsible for making you
46 Gran Ford models
50 Prayer ending
52 "_____ beautiful day in the neighborhood"
54 Drug cop
55 Fruity confection with a streusel topping
59 Capital on the Nile
61 Montreal baseball team
62 Chaney of horror movies
63 Out of style
64 With _____ in sight
65 Quarterback Manning
66 Remains of fires
67 Peruvian peaks
68 "Just a _____ "

1 Vowel sound of "lets" and "bets"
2 Moray hunters
3 On _____ (precisely)
4 _____ de Colombier, St. Barts
5 Vend
6 Doesn't turn off
7 Ciao, in Paris
8 Repeated chant
9 Kate of *The Martian*
10 Similar
11 One who abandons
12 Exist
13 Peaks: Abbr.
21 Broadcasting giant
22 Wakes up after being unconscious
26 _____ one's loins
27 Add- _____ (extras)
29 Nodded off
30 Of the great seas
32 Modify
35 _____ up your sleeve
37 Of the great seas
38 To's opposite
39 Pilaf or paella
40 Not yet used
41 Spy org.
45 Goddess of wisdom and war
47 Italian city near Vesuvius
48 Player on a Baltimore team
49 Picturesque
51 Breastfeed
53 Anglo- _____
56 _____ the line
57 Corn _____
58 Mind-blowing drugs: Abbr.
59 Tax professional in Apr.
60 Small batteries

SWEETS

1	2	3	■	4	5	6	7	8	■	9	10	11	12	13
14			■	15					■	16				
17			■	18					■	19				
20			21					22					■	■
23				■	24				■	25		26	27	
28				29	30		31		32		■	33		
■	■	34				35	■	36		37				■
■	38	39				40								■
41					■	42					■	■	■	■
43			■	44	45		46				47	48	49	
50			51	■	52	53		■	54					
■	55		56				57	58						
59	60			■	61				■	62				
63				■	64				■	65				
66				■	67				■	68				

ACROSS

1 Photo _____ (publicity events)
4 "One small _____ for man . . ."
8 Capital of Eritrea
14 Empty words
15 Adios, in Italy
16 Safari sights
17 _____ -Pen (essential for the allergic)
18 Strong flavor of a sauce for beef
20 Chocolate source
22 "Able was I _____ I saw Elba"
23 "Got it!"
24 Herb in Thai soups
28 "If all _____ fails . . ."
29 Romantic dinner lights
34 Old Russian ruler
37 "On a wing _____ prayer"
40 Hawaiian patio
41 Caprese greenery
43 Web address
44 Secret meeting
45 *A Town Like* _____ (book by Nevil Shute)
46 Chair part
48 Syrup sources
49 Feast
51 True
53 Bagel topping
58 GI off base
62 Allow
63 Peepers
65 Source of a popular extract
69 Narrow inlet
70 Suit for a baby
71 _____ and Crafts (architectural style)
72 Verb suffix
73 Empty _____ (one whose kids have moved away)
74 Family chart
75 Barely make

DOWN

1 Oil grp.
2 Vatican-related
3 "Variety is the _____ of life" (subject of this crossword)
4 College
5 Uncle, in Cancún
6 Knack for music
7 Faker
8 Apprehend
9 _____ Na Na
10 Modest skirt length
11 Licorice flavoring in Spain
12 Pink wine
13 Arthur of the courts
19 Historic age
21 Land of the free
25 Fort Meade grp.
26 It's Pongo for orangutans
27 Seasoning all creatures need
30 Green accent to Italian dishes
31 "Orinoco Flow" singer
32 Grate
33 Takes a break
34 Old ski lift
35 Discount event
36 "Take _____ " (taste)
38 Dr. of rap
39 Scare
42 Lower
47 Golf ball lifter
50 Bank clerk
52 _____ of urgency (haste)
54 Celtic is one
55 Up during the game
56 Creepy
57 Cocktail
58 Stratford's river
59 Ebb
60 9 is in this column in $49.12
61 Tally
64 Aromatic in stuffing
66 Untruth
67 "To _____ is human"
68 Dined

ZEST

ACROSS

1 Pear with a warm cinnamon color
5 At a distance
9 Friendly greeting
14 Woody Guthrie's son
15 Bitter
16 Yellow-to-brown earth pigment
17 Title princess who eats her stepmother's poisoned apple
19 Be in hot water?
20 Toga-party staple
21 Unagi or anago at a sushi bar
22 Asparagus or pickle servings
24 Wipes clean
26 Like some grapes and watermelons
28 Daly with three consecutive Emmys for *Cagney & Lacey*
29 Tempest in a teapot
30 Chicken tender?
31 French _____
34 Automat or pizzeria, e.g.
37 Title wizard who eats Bertie Bott's Every Flavour Beans and drinks Butterbeer
39 _____ pig (South American rodent with an African name)
41 Tests
42 Make a choice
43 iPod model smaller than a Mini
45 Moussaka meat
49 Disaster that may not be covered by insurance
52 Capture the heart of
54 More frilly
55 A-Rod fiancée and former *American Idol* judge
56 Cool _____ cucumber
57 Prize that Sartre compared to "a sack of potatoes"
58 Title killjoy who shares roast beast with his reindeer-dressed dog, Max
61 Religion that disallows the eating of pork
62 German export with a Latin name
63 Khloé Kardashian ex Lamar
64 Decade that first saw the Cronut and the Impossible Burger
65 Leg part
66 Lumberjacks' tools

DOWN

1 Picnic carrier
2 Pig-headed
3 "Taste the rainbow," e.g.
4 Milk producer
5 Cookout leftovers?
6 Food wrap
7 Oldenburg's *Apple Core* or Warhol's *Campbell's Soup Cans,* e.g.
8 Pieces seen in *E.T. the Extra-Terrestrial*
9 Flimflammed
10 Base 8
11 Anyplace
12 Bedroom furniture piece
13 "You bet!"
18 Pint-sized
23 Paella-purchasing currency replaced by the euro
25 Family car
26 Discontinue temporarily
27 Place for a pig
29 Cook, as bacon
32 Source of iron
33 Fruit or its namesake color
35 Dough dispenser
36 Make of the first car in space (Elon Musk's own)
37 Like pitches batters love
38 Good Grips kitchen-utensil brand
39 Make a little _____ long way
40 Very near
44 Major blood vessels
46 Actress Plummer or Seyfried
47 National capital in which one might try borscht or blini
48 Lullaby composer Johannes
50 _____ Spray (inventors of the juice box)
51 *Chocolat* and *Wild Strawberries,* e.g.
52 NBA legend Baylor
53 Neither fish _____ fowl
55 *Star Wars: The Last* _____
57 Something to pick
59 "What?"
60 Apple mobile platform

CONSUMER REPORTS

ACROSS

1 Like aged cheddar cheese
6 Kitchen sight
10 Young socialites
14 Type of lunch or tie
15 Bryn _____ College
16 "Pronto!"
17 Cream-filled, ganache-topped oblong of choux pastry
20 Early ISP
21 Carbonation
22 Television show genre
23 Hindu title of respect
24 Bikini part
25 Flaky, yeast-leavened curved pastry
34 Fireplace residue
35 Trick
36 Canonized figure, in Brazil
37 Appears to be
38 Home of the Tar Heels
39 Florida theme park
41 Judge who oversaw the O.J. Simpson trial
42 Carrie's *Star Wars* role
43 Orange Bowl city
44 Tropical fruit–flavored crusted dessert with a custardy filling
48 Many Apple devices run on it
49 Genetic messenger material
50 Some reds
54 Air safety org.
55 Lobster eater's accessory
58 Layered dessert made with devil's food sponge, whipped topping and cherries
61 Simple aquatic plant
62 Single item
63 Stand in a studio
64 Spotted
65 Connecticut town for which a tick-borne disease is named
66 Unlawfully take

DOWN

1 Pet protection grp.
2 Hostess snack cake
3 Military truant
4 Button on a DVR
5 Move forward
6 Recording-artist honors ceremony held each Nov. in Nashville
7 Lid
8 Fancy pitcher
9 Giveaway
10 Cowboys' home
11 Actor Morales
12 Fish tempter
13 Surprisingly nimble
18 Den
19 These can cause congestion
23 Cherry feature
25 Elementary
26 Be of _____ (assist)
27 2000s Fox drama set in Southern California
28 Salad dressing holder
29 Like some ancient alphabets
30 Grouchy Muppet
31 BMI alternative
32 Supermodel Campbell
33 1960s comedienne and singer Fields
39 Arises (from)
40 Quality cotton
42 Libidinous
45 Tin Woodman's request
46 Breakfast area
47 Time periods
50 Wall St. degrees
51 Fashion magazine
52 Frenzy
53 Competitor of 1-Across
54 Fancy party
55 Acid neutralizer
56 Furniture chain
57 Type of pepper
59 Lip
60 Food Network star Cora

A VISIT TO THE BAKERY

1	2	3	4	5	■	6	7	8	9	■	10	11	12	13
14					■	15				■	16			
17				18					19				
20			■	21			■	22				■	■
■	■	23				■		24			■	■	■
25	26	27			28	29	30			31	32	33
34				■	35			■		36		
37				■	38			■	39	40		
41			■	42				■	43		
44		45	46			47			
■	■	48			■	49			■	■
50	51	52		53	■	54		■	55	56	57
58				59			60		
61			■	62		■	63		
64			■	65		■	66		

1 Some precipitation
5 Make untidy
9 Powder mineral
13 The duck in *Peter and the Wolf*
14 Japan's second-largest city
16 Where more than half the world lives
17 What split seafood shall we grill?
20 Greek vowel
21 Valley
22 Legendary strongman
23 Anointing liquid
24 One brand of this foodstuff has a mermaid for a logo
25 What filled "other white meat" shall we grill?
33 Like a pig's tail
34 Movie parts
35 SNL alum Gasteyer
36 Napoleon's exile site
37 Sign on a restroom
38 Heap for ceremonial burning
39 Govt. code-breaking group
40 Fad
41 "Later!"
42 What marinated poultry shall we grill?
45 Off-color, or perhaps blue
46 Sitcom planet
47 In a mechanical manner of learning
50 Classic board game
52 Some Panasonic products
55 What tender cut of beef shall we grill?
58 Shade trees often lining streets
59 Hitched
60 Prefix with present or bus
61 Like a busybody
62 Writes
63 Frank

1 Health-club wrap
2 Share a border with
3 Bit
4 Cook's hair wear
5 Group spirit
6 Pro sports league from 1983 to 1986
7 Attraction for shoppers
8 What's up
9 Airport surface
10 "Buyer beware" warning
11 Fancy wheels
12 Cereal mascot honorific
15 Gives confidence to
18 Enlighten
19 Yarn units
23 *Man _____ Mancha*
24 Pre-Aztec Indian
25 Aroma
26 Oklahoma city
27 Like city folk
28 Dismal
29 1920s schemer
30 Kahlo portrayer
31 Sandwich specification
32 Song of praise
37 Where to get supplies for your cookout
38 Part of a bushel
40 Raccoon relative
41 Horse dads
43 Full of impurities
44 Pursues doggedly
47 Alphanumeric vitamin also known as PABA
48 "Go for it!" acronym
49 Tachometer readings: Abbr.
50 Soft drink option
51 Security interest
52 Fill-in
53 Barn-top sight
54 What cracklings are made from
56 Dock
57 This many cooks spoil the broth, proverbially

BACKYARD BARBECUE

1 Inter _____
5 Piece of diced ham, essentially
9 Small silvery fish
14 It's often brought by a waiter
15 Computer operating system developed in the 1960s
16 Otherworldly
17 She had #1 hits with "Tennessee Waltz" and "The Doggie in the Window"
19 Historical record
20 Small appliance that slices and blends
22 Chowder chewable
23 Eponymous restaurateur and "trader"
24 Small appliance that brews and steams
32 Forward
33 Salmon, for example
34 Opposite of oui
35 Splinter group
36 Mint brand
38 Skillful
39 Time period
40 Pieces of information
41 New person at the office
42 Small appliance that browns and melts
46 Unit of corn
47 Bruins' home
48 Small appliance that heats and reheats
54 Typeface flourish
55 Forms a scab, perhaps
57 Stage whisper, perhaps
58 Folk singer Woody's son
59 Start and end of a race, proverbially
60 Stunned, in a way
61 Highly recommend
62 Food on the farm

1 Roadie's responsibility
2 Tree feature
3 Fond of
4 Overlord
5 Tea servings, in Britain
6 Takes weapons from
7 Nickname of NBA Hall of Famer Oscar Robertson
8 Company VIP
9 In need of Dramamine, perhaps
10 All-around good guy
11 Puzzle inventor Rubik
12 Fabricator
13 Abbr. on a business card
18 Killed time
21 Author George Eliot's last name, at birth
24 Mitigates
25 He-Man's twin sister
26 Popular pie option
27 Media star known primarily by her first name
28 Cambridge school that hosts the annual Mystery Hunt puzzle weekend, in brief
29 Not active or reactive
30 Lacking an initial or periodic charge, like some checking accounts
31 Key keyboard key
36 Large African city nicknamed "The City of a Thousand Minarets"
37 List-ending abbreviation
38 Denies knowledge of
40 Towered over
41 Saintly symbols
43 Resolve
44 Polynesian island country with the valuable Internet domain suffix .tv
45 Spotted cat
48 Small plateau
49 It's in the eye of the beholder
50 Second-baseman in an Abbott and Costello routine
51 Nestlé chocolate bar with a frothy texture
52 Its existence has been the subject of much debate among theologians
53 Tyrannical Roman emperor
54 Did not rise
56 Part of a set in the gym

SMALL APPLIANCES

ACROSS

1 1975 Spielberg blockbuster
5 Tea drink with tapioca pearls
9 Expression of relief
13 Found a perch
14 Stylized crime dramas
15 Volcano output
16 Handy device for prepping carrots and cucumbers
19 State with authority
20 Bakes, in a way
21 Impactful to one's sense of sight or hearing
23 Japanese drama
24 Handy set when following a recipe
32 Sep. follower
33 Long-snouted rhino relative
34 Swashbuckler Flynn
35 Prescribed amount
37 Brand identifiers
39 Ann's advisory sister
40 She was nominated and confirmed next after Sonia
42 Hotelier Helmsley
44 Martinique, *par exemple*
45 Handy device for properly cooking roasts
48 Central word in a palindrome about Napoleon
49 Patriot missile's target
50 Residents of Fars Province
55 Common panini cheese
59 Handy pair of devices for making tasty pastes like pesto or guacamole
61 Ballet move
62 Many jazz combos
63 Arabian Peninsula sultanate
64 Gets
65 Promotion
66 He was lost and found in a 2003 film

DOWN

1 Morning mugful
2 Pub choices
3 Covers for domes
4 Braces (oneself)
5 Short do
6 Vinaigrette necessities
7 Steep
8 Common ski slope trees
9 Abundance
10 Sound
11 Word appearing three times in a row, as an intensifier, in the lyrics of a 2012 Taylor Swift song
12 Hawks favor them
14 Not artificial
17 Lake fish often served amandine
18 Get married without an affair
22 Pair of equal and opposite electric charges considered as a unit
24 Internet on-ramp, in a way
25 Place to learn in Lyon
26 Confused
27 African country or river
28 Stablehands, often
29 Typically elliptical path
30 Like some elemental gases
31 More crafty
36 International accords
38 Nestlé candy brand
41 Open courtyards
43 Emulate a jester
46 Fireside
47 Founder of General Electric
50 Little devils
51 Function or capacity
52 Singer India
53 Not even, quaintly
54 Quick cut
56 "Look _____ , I'm Sandra Dee" (*Grease* song)
57 Bowie's rock genre
58 Wine: Prefix
60 Buck's counterpart

USEFUL UTENSILS

ACROSS

ACROSS

1 Helpful hints
5 Concede
10 Scary Spice, to friends
14 Early man
15 TV executive Arledge
16 Baseball's Moisés or Felipe
17 Small, tapered green vegetables
20 Operatic piece
21 Lead-in to cycle or verse
22 Japanese computer giant
23 Vine vegetable with orange flesh
28 401(k) alternative
29 Damage beyond repair
30 "That's delicious!"
31 Edible flatfish
33 Coalesces
35 O.K. Corral lawman
38 *Vogue* competitor
39 Ice cream serving
41 Actress Ward of *The Fugitive*
43 Sewing junction
45 Beige shade
46 Future plant
47 What a basketball basket is attached to
49 Held on to
51 Pop
52 Small, round green vegetables
57 Unagi, at a sushi bar
58 x/x (unless x is zero)
59 Fair-hiring watchdog org.
60 Baseball-sized red vegetable
66 Fried egg option
67 Yellow-orange shade or pigment
68 School fundraising grps.
69 Cancún currency
70 Bright and reflective
71 Present

DOWN

1 _____Mahal
2 Actress Lupino
3 Pleasing to the taste
4 Hurt
5 They lie around the house
6 Put on
7 Pasture sound
8 Data fed to a computer
9 Small in a big way
10 Meteorologist's aid
11 Supreme Court Justice Kagan
12 Bodies of knowledge or traditions
13 Big name in brewing
18 Docking site
19 Excite, as curiosity
23 Patiently wait
24 Range dividing Europe and Asia
25 Typically younger relative
26 Uses a key on, often
27 Amherst school, informally
32 Locks in the juices, on a grill
34 Painful places
36 Teach good habits to replace bad ones
37 Fold that's worn
40 Manipulation of Kermit or Miss Piggy, for example
42 Mixes in
44 Some Asian soups
48 Impulse purchase advertised as "The Freshmaker"
50 BlackBerry rival introduced by Palm in 2002
52 Jazz genre
53 Pilgrim in *The Canterbury Tales*
54 _____Gold (Peter Fonda film)
55 Moocher
56 Extra gusto
61 To's partner
62 Yellowfin tuna
63 Sphere of knowledge
64 Steamroller's target, often
65 Sugary suffix

(NOTE: Some theme entries are botanically classified as fruits, but all would be at home in a vegetable garden.)

VEGETABLE GARDEN

1 Ark contents
6 List bullet
10 "Right away!" in a hospital
14 Beethoven dedicatee
15 Animated explorer
16 No more than
17 Author of *30-Minute Meals*
19 Fired
20 Science guy Bill
21 Colors eggs for Easter
22 Piano size
23 Author of *Cooking for Friends*
26 Apple store purchase
29 Equine morsel
30 Politico Romney
31 Smoothie ingredient
33 Rx overseer
36 Author of *Kitchen Confidential*
40 Doze
41 Cass Elliot and Michelle Phillips in the 1960s
42 Hot spot
43 Pollution watchdog org.
44 Copy illegally
46 Author of *Modern French Cooking for the American Kitchen*
52 *Carmen,* for example
53 1980 Irene Cara movie and song
54 Crummy grade
57 Part of a 1492 trio
58 Author of *Mastering the Art of French Cooking*
61 "_____ one, purl two"
62 Country northeast of Yemen
63 Seating option
64 Strong desires
65 Has
66 _____ pie

1 Gull cousin
2 Skin-care brand
3 Houston university
4 Former ember
5 Like some collisions
6 Ran without moving
7 Human trunk
8 Tide competitor
9 Kentucky Derby month
10 False flattery
11 Austin's home
12 Rock concert venue
13 _____ bear
18 Bronte's Jane
22 Croc kin
23 Gloomy look
24 Forbidden acts
25 Prego rival
26 Somalian supermodel
27 _____ colada
28 URL start
31 "Dude!"
32 Attorneys' org.
33 Falafel bean
34 Lose on purpose
35 Princess born in 1950
37 Last Greek letter
38 County east of Sonoma
39 *The Big Bang Theory* type
44 Cat that's also a sneaker brand
45 Global-warming concern
46 Like an expert in arcana
47 Pontificate
48 Occupant of a Red Square tomb
49 Keg party throwers, frequently
50 F-sharp
51 Annoyances
54 Part of CD-ROM
55 First name in scat
56 First place?
58 Coffee
59 Thurman of the *Kill Bill* movies
60 Hurry, old-style

CHEFS AND THEIR BOOKS

1 Overly sentimental
6 Nailed
10 Bros, e.g.
14 Sunlit lobbies
15 Willing and able
16 Singer-songwriter Amos
17 Edible 2000 animated movie with the voice of Mel Gibson
19 Universal donor's blood type, briefly
20 Egg producers
21 Spike or Ang
22 Extraterrestrial
23 Verb that's an anagram of its past tense
24 Edible 1988 romantic comedy starring Julia Roberts
27 Roman fountain
29 Treasure location indicator, perhaps
30 Long, skinny fish
31 Online troublemaker
33 _____-relief
34 Throws in
35 Edible 2004 crime drama starring Daniel Craig
38 Jest
41 Nutritional stat.
42 Makes out, to a Brit
45 Stud location
46 Fish part
47 Gourmet mushroom
49 Edible 1999 comedy starring Jason Biggs
54 Apple's Cook
55 On the up-and-up
56 Dubious ability, for short
57 Dove product
58 Designer Cassini
59 Edible 2006 comedy starring Jack Black
62 Reverse
63 Black-and-white sea creature
64 Dancing dizzily
65 Crystal ball user
66 Feline's "Feed me!"
67 King with a golden touch

1 Scented pouch
2 Deep down inside
3 Epson product
4 Photos
5 Shaggy grazer
6 Dancer de Mille
7 ^
8 Ostrich cousin
9 Television location, frequently
10 Vodka brand, for short
11 Missing some electrons
12 Took care of easily, with "through"
13 Cues
18 Actor Ron who played Tarzan
22 *Fortnite,* for example
24 Leon Uris's _____ *18*
25 Apple introduction of 1998
26 Oaxacan houses
28 Meadow rodent
32 "There's a lady who's sure all that glitters is gold," for example
33 Sports _____
34 Very long time
36 Funny Dame
37 Patella location
38 Resentful of someone else's success
39 *Winnie-the-Pooh* author
40 Come before
43 Hit the hay
44 Tahoe's Squaw Valley, for example
46 In shape
48 Pushes forward
50 Discipline
51 Wafer brand
52 "Nonsense!"
53 Big news on Wall St.
57 "Hey _____" (start of some phone calls)
59 Pierre or Yvette
60 Word sometimes abbreviated by its middle letter in texts
61 Escapee's flight

EDIBLE MOVIES

1	2	3	4	5	■	6	7	8	9	■	10	11	12	13
14						15					16			
17				18							19			
20				■	21			■		22				
23			■	24				25	26					
27			28		■			29			■	30		
■	31				32		33				34			
■			35		36				37		■			
38	39	40		■	41			42			43	44	■	
45			■	46			■			47				48
49			50			51	52	53		■	54			
55				■		56			■	57				
58			■	59	60				61					
62			■	63			■		64					
65			■	66			■		67					

1 Pop-up paths
5 State between Washington and Montana
10 Chooses
14 Mound
15 Music mixer's knob
16 Small salamander
17 Place to get a new iPhone
19 Prime draft status
20 One whose pants are on fire?
21 Biceps location
22 Commonly
23 Volkswagen introduction of 1979
24 Teenage boy's facial hair, perhaps
26 When a flight is due in, for short
27 Erie Canal mule
29 Negative vote
30 Cause of a princess's sleepless night?
31 Liberty_____
33 Cartographer's drawing
35 Small dog, briefly
37 University of California, Santa Cruz, athletes
41 The _____ (musical set in Oz)
42 Regret
43 Leonardo's _____ Lisa
46 The Braves, on scoreboards
49 Chicken on a French restaurant menu
51 To the _____ degree
53 Actress Courteney of Friends
54 Post cereal offering
57 Banded rock
59 Person who needs good boots
60 "Look at the pretty fireworks!"
61 Underground tunneler
62 State emphatically
63 What you get by combining the beginnings of 17-, 24-, 37- and 54-Across
66 Madams' counterparts
67 "Close,_____ cigar"
68 Mexican money
69 Zap, in a way
70 "No more for me, thanks"
71 Ben & Jerry's competitor

1 "I understand now"
2 Filled (with)
3 Beginning of Brazil?
4 Sound of a watermelon hitting concrete
5 No _____ , ands or buts
6 Verizon offering
7 Love like crazy
8 Moby-Dick writer Melville
9 Mine find
10 Switch words
11 Like some emotions
12 Pluck, in a way
13 Poem section
18 Significant periods
22 "Stop kidding around!"
23 Former Florida governor Bush
25 Pill shape
28 Large e-tailer
32 Murphy's _____
34 It's usually 3, 4 or 5
36 Studio with a roaring lion mascot
38 Less like an ogre
39 Part of a clear weather forecast
40 Supposed
44 Difficult
45 Thing to grind?
46 Shocked
47 Quiz show material
48 Los Angeles cagers
50 Enough members to vote
52 Bad actors
55 In and of itself
56 Promotes
58 Really flip out
63 The X-Files org.
64 Wee one
65 Two, in Oaxaca

FARMERS' MARKET

1 Pastrami purveyor
5 International call for help
11 Basic cable channel
14 "Terrible" ruler
15 One-celled protozoa
16 Computer in *2001*
17 *Rebel Without a Cause* director
19 Peeper
20 Keyboard interval
21 Guys
22 Blender setting
23 Swindled
24 Baseball player with the largest sports contract in history
26 Complimentary
28 Swedish car company
29 Shareable computer file, for short
32 Famous _____ (cookie brand)
35 Earth tone
38 Best-selling author of young-adult thrillers
42 ESPN replay technique
43 Goulash, e.g.
44 X
45 Cry from the crib
47 Sweetheart
50 Former 'N Sync member
54 Substantial
58 God of love
59 Keats creation
60 "No argument here"
61 Solemn promise
62 Classical guitarist with multiple Grammys
64 Angsty rock genre
65 Luke's father in *Star Wars*
66 To be: Latin
67 Was in charge of
68 Figures of speech
69 As a result

1 *Jurassic Park* creatures, for short
2 Throw out
3 Milk: Prefix
4 Divided 50/50
5 Like stallions
6 Doctors' grp.
7 *Mario Kart* character
8 Bo of *10*
9 Humiliates
10 Triumphant cry
11 Tolkien tale
12 Crocodile habitat
13 Rested
18 In the past
22 Painful spasm
24 Written reminders
25 Bull: Prefix
27 Have dinner
29 Alternatives to 39-Down
30 FedEx competitor
31 Henceforth
33 Make a decision
34 Backyard structures
36 Barely make, with "out"
37 Stimpy's pal
39 Apple products since 1998
40 Not all
41 Female in a flock
46 Be plentiful
48 Melville captain
49 Feel sorry about
50 Bar for lifting
51 Fragrance
52 1950s candidate Stevenson
53 Omega rival
55 Straight from the garden
56 Tantalize
57 Aden is its largest city
60 Resting places
62 _____ alai
63 Intention

CATCH OF THE DAY

1 The "A." in Thomas A. Edison
5 Israeli leader Shimon
10 Cracked a little
14 Symbol of control
15 Praise highly
16 Sheltered spot
17 Singer with the 1996 triple-platinum album *Tidal*
19 Not 42-Across
20 Slowly, musically
21 Stopping point
23 Member of a colony
24 Pequod, for one
26 Tim Roth's *Reservoir Dogs* role
28 Chow
29 Kind of baseball game
30 Title holder
32 Dude
33 Wrapped up
34 Act lovey-dovey
35 1985 role for Christopher Lloyd
40 Patriots' grp.
41 Days, in Durango
42 At this time
44 Hazards at sea
47 *America's Got Talent* judge, for short
48 Bit of dialogue
49 Tina Fey's character on *30 Rock*
51 Fancy neckwear
53 *Mogambo* actress Gardner
54 Bit of skin art, slangily
55 Culinary creation
56 Insignificant
58 Charter member of the Rock & Roll Hall of Fame
62 Fraternal group since 1868
63 Start of a children's rhyme
64 Drug addict
65 The "S" in GPS: Abbr.
66 Kind of code
67 Farm enclosures

1 Canine cry
2 Floral necklace
3 Rule breaker, e.g.
4 Historical records
5 Small rocks in a walkway
6 Trade show
7 Knock lightly
8 Mystery author Queen
9 Dictation expert
10 One of two in *Hamilton*
11 Strauss or Bach
12 Get even
13 One paying a flat fee
18 The Doors' "People _____ Strange"
22 Yields to gravity
24 Halloween decoration
25 Zither's cousin
26 James of *X-Men* films
27 Way off base?
30 *Rushmore* director Anderson
33 Compensate for
34 Maryland seafood fare
36 First year at law school
37 Refinery input
38 Cosmologist's concern
39 Lisa with a "mystic smile"
43 Kind of bar
44 Heartthrobs
45 Spirited
46 Missouri mountains
47 May honoree
48 Tie, as sneakers
50 Sprayed, defensively
52 Soothe, as sore muscles
55 Chem. and bio.
57 Clock setting in NYC
59 One, on the Oise
60 Stimpy's cartoon pal
61 Mos. turn into them

FRUIT BASKET

1 Priority Mail org.
5 She, in Sicily
9 Network for Alexandria Ocasio-Cortez
14 Marie Curie, for one
15 Bottle in a pharmacy, perhaps
16 Boy band formed in 2000 that was sued by a Detroit-based record label because the names were too similar
17 Machine in a casino
18 109 for meitnerium, say
19 Honkers
20 2012 French movie filmed in part at the Palais de l'Élysée while the French president was away
23 One of the noble gases
24 *Nip/Tuck* instrument
28 Baby's cry
29 First word in "Jabberwocky"
33 Plan of sorts
34 R-E-S-P-E-C-T singer
36 Falco of *Nurse Jackie*
37 1987 Danish movie that won the Oscar for Best Foreign Language Film
41 Sauce brand founded in 1937
42 Ridiculous
43 Ω Ω Ω
46 Hathaway or Hathaway
47 End of many a company name
50 Mastermind behind Caesar's assassination, according to Shakespeare
52 Drink with Mayan roots
54 2001 British movie featuring Gordon Ramsay as a supporting actor
58 Common ACME product
61 Defeat decisively
62 Big name in DVRs
63 Genre for Octavia E. Butler
64 Big name in Pods
65 One in 66-Across
66 Midwest mnemonic
67 It was once believed to be indivisible
68 Tattled

1 Footballer Gene who played in the Super Bowl for the Oakland Raiders in three different decades
2 Toyota coupe from 1999 to 2008
3 Start to prepare a field, in England
4 Fight
5 Get out: Abbr.
6 It means "place" in Latin
7 _____-Flush (bygone cleanser)
8 At _____ (confused)
9 Alternative to dessert
10 Trout that's the state fish of Washington
11 Edgar Allan whose Baltimore home is now a (tiny) museum
12 Comments heard around a cute baby, perhaps
13 Atlanta to Pittsburgh direction
21 _____ nous (just between us)
22 CPUs, e.g.
25 Crosswalk walkers, briefly
26 Send out
27 Harper who wrote *Go Set a Watchman*
30 Not dry
31 _____ -girl
32 Biblical queen's realm
34 Pixar movie featuring Julia Louis-Dreyfus
35 Org.
37 The Crimson Tide, to fans
38 Ice, Stone, Bronze, Iron, etc.
39 First word in the first crossword puzzle in 1913
40 Build, say
41 Mythical bird
44 Typically garlicky sauces
45 Subaru Ascent, for one
47 Longtime Seattle Mariners outfielder who started his career with the Orix BlueWave
48 What one of the monkeys saw
49 Paddled
51 Sealy competitor
53 Group of eight
55 "And _____ goes"
56 Tribute
57 One on an agenda
58 Pokémon trainer known as Satoshi in Japan
59 Sgt., e.g.
60 Vigor's partner

GET TO THE POPCORN

1 Joe Fejes, winner of 2019's Six Days in the Dome, has run 133 of them
5 On or about
10 Possesses
14 "Yeah, right"
15 Danny played by George Clooney and Frank Sinatra
16 One producing a lot of feet
17 Just
18 Intended
19 Stylish, perhaps
20 Song made famous by Fats Domino that was often featured on *Happy Days*
23 Auction item
24 Alternative to 12-Down
25 Agcy. featured prominently in *Breaking Bad*
28 Almost every monitor sold these days
31 Booker T. & the M.G.'s blues rock song of 1962, one of the most popular instrumental rock and soul songs ever
35 *Cat on _____ Tin Roof*
37 Web address
38 Elba who played Mandela
39 Buds
40 "Weird Al" Yankovic song of 1984 and an alternative title for this puzzle
43 A coin rarely lands on one
44 Journalist Farrow
46 _____ Kosh B'gosh
47 A school year typically has two
48 Don McLean song from 1971
52 Dorm supervisors
53 Some receivers: Abbr.
54 Group with Sharks, Ducks and Panthers
55 Monopoly has four
57 Song based on a 1911 poem by James Oppenheim, sung at Mount Holyoke College during graduation
64 Like 64-Across
66 Wanderer
67 It's just the way it's going to be
68 Mostly bygone stamp feature: Abbr.
69 Joe quantity
70 Prong
71 Name in organic frozen foods
72 You might write one to get into college
73 Applaud

1 Branch
2 Biblical brother
3 Tegucigalpa : Honduras :: Lima : _____
4 Metal that Superman isn't actually made of
5 Get real?
6 Decorator of sorts
7 Behind
8 There's a Grand one in the U.S. Southwest
9 The study of the human race, briefly
10 Grandmother in the *Pickles* comic strip
11 It was said we got a new one after the Cold War
12 Alternative to 24-Across
13 Pigpen
21 Slow (down)
22 Fire: Prefix
26 Conundrum
27 Determine
28 Research subject
29 Google's browser
30 First comic strip to win a Pulitzer
32 Constitutional amendment first introduced in Congress in 1923
33 "Rocket Man" John
34 They're famously in March
36 Loser of 1917
41 One way to access the Web
42 According to the International Organization for Standardization, it's Wednesday, not Tuesday
45 *Brooklyn Nine-_____*
49 1 in 1,000, perhaps
50 English writer and philosopher Huxley
51 Make a mistake
56 Calcium has one, not two
58 Game officials
59 Band equipment
60 County adjacent to Sonoma
61 Pilot a boat, perhaps
62 One of the world's most active volcanoes
63 Flow (through)
64 Tax preparer, at times
65 Writer Stanisław with an asteroid named after him

LISTEN

ACROSS

1 Obama adviser Emanuel
5 Nothing
8 Country with 6,852 islands
13 Alternate name
15 Make (out)
16 What a meter might read
17 Overspice the Indian food?
20 "Whatever you'd like"
21 Condo grp.
22 ____ -cone
23 Sought, as an office
27 Used to be
30 A note left with the bill, perhaps?
33 One in the WNBA draft
34 Instructed
35 L
36 One in the Battle of Hastings
39 School where Kofi Annan got his master's in management
40 Lift
41 Offer enticement to
42 Warren Buffett, famously
44 Greek god of war
45 Error of putting the wrong herb on pasta?
49 Director Howard
50 Numbered button on a car radio
51 Member of the Big 12
52 Consume
53 Observer of sorts
56 What the chef might have after prepping the steak?
62 Marilyn Monroe's real first name
63 Mo. without any U.S. holidays
64 Quarrel
65 Journalist and writer Faludi who won the Pulitzer and Kirkus Prizes
66 You can't fit a square one into a round hole
67 Some recipe amts.

DOWN

1 Certain discrimination
2 Barack and Michelle Obama, to Harvard
3 Join a company
4 NPR's Liasson
5 Central figure in *The Matrix*
6 Presidential candidate of 1952
7 *The Joy of* ____ (a book about language)
8 One of twelve, typically
9 Hopelessly lost
10 Jenna played her on *The Office*
11 70, for a septuagenarian
12 Early game console
14 The S in GPS
18 Alpine region in Austria
19 You, way back when
24 Kobe Bryant's hometown in Pennsylvania
25 "The Gray Lady"
26 Measurement for a film reel
27 How many connect to the Internet
28 A Shakespearean play has five
29 Actor Ione
31 Sports car features popular in the '60s and '70s
32 Helvetica or Palatino
33 88-keyed instrument
35 She played with Kukla and Ollie on TV
36 Mariska Hargitay, vis-à-vis *Law & Order: SVU*
37 Inflated British chocolate bar
38 Marvel-ous mutants
43 Troll on the Internet
45 "____ take arms against a sea of troubles": *Hamlet*
46 Burns
47 Frozen like a road in winter
48 Brings back to health
50 Joyful hymn
52 Jane Austen novel of 1815
54 '50s group ____ Na Na
55 Role in a play
56 Wts. that shipping containers are measured in
57 The Astros, on the scoreboard
58 There are 1,000 in a millennium
59 Catch some z's
60 Tint
61 One might be deviled

ACROSS

1 Mexican houses
6 City by the Bay force
10 "It's _____ "
14 Cheri of *SNL*
15 Trim down
16 Close to
17 Stainless, say
18 Sea with a Scrabble score of 16 (if proper names were allowed, that is)
19 Traveled by horse, perhaps
20 The clambake caterer relied on her . . .
23 Chant
24. If you're punctual, you might be on it
28 Mary Barra at General Motors
29. Almost all are flat-screen, these days
31 Force felt at blastoff
32 How a company goes public
33 The salad maker messed up when she . . .
36 Start of a magic word
39 Grain in many a gluten-free cereal
40 Reader since 1984
41 The expert sommelier belonged to the . . .
46 Hot item in a newsroom
47 Rainier or Denali: Abbr.
48 One in a series
49 Eggs in a laboratory
52 Street on PBS
54 Layered
56 The Indian baker was careful to follow the . . .
60 Setting for a phaser on *Star Trek*
63 A complete outfit, say
64 Cars
65 Seaweed-wrapped roll in Japan
66 Only U.S. president to also serve as a Supreme Court justice
67 Prefix meaning "image," not to be confused with the prefix meaning "cheap"
68 "Yup"
69 Toques and porkpies
70 Showed again

DOWN

1 "Out there"
2 Bring into agreement
3 Handles, as a handler might
4 "You _____ Beautiful" (Joe Cocker song)
5 Property of a Knight, but not a King
6 Most e-mail, sadly
7 Rattle
8 High school gala
9 How Sandy felt hopelessly about Danny in *Grease*
10 How a Reuben is usually served
11 Central character in *The Matrix*
12 Humor magazine founded in 1952
13 Central word in a famous palindrome
21 Strauss who founded the eponymous clothing company
22 She played Carla on *Cheers*
25 Word before Coke or Pepsi
26 Word on a store sign
27 Canvas bag, say
30 A runcible one is also a fork
31 Arrive, as on a flight
33 Maple syrup, basically
34 Major election force
35 Stock market action
36 The CIA and FBI have them
37 Gooey cheese
38 50 Cent pieces?
42 Stone of *Birdman*
43 Ninja strong suit
44 James of song
45 How one might vanish?
49 Speaker
50 Setting for *Romeo and Juliet*
51 Builds an extension, say
53 Broadway musical that premiered in 1977
55 Coax out
57 Weather map org.
58 p, on a piano score
59 Times Square booth or an abbreviation of what they sell
60 Text message tech
61 Letter between Σ and Υ
62 Country embroiled in a 2019 Trump administration scandal: Abbr.

THE CHEF

ANSWER KEY

RECIPE REPAIRS

Tomato and Avocado Salad with Green Goddess Dressing

Yield: The salad serves 4 people, not 40.

Ingredients: The recipe uses sour cream, not sour crème fraîche.

Ingredients: The garlic clove should be peeled.

Ingredients: You're using basil leaves, not flowers.

Ingredients: You'll need to dice the avocado before adding it to the salad.

Ingredients: The recipe needs 1 pint of cherry tomatoes, not just 1 tomato.

Step 1: At 550°F, the oven is too hot and the almonds will burn. The correct temperature is 350°F.

Step 2: The mayonnaise has been omitted from the recipe. Add it to the blender or food processor with the buttermilk and sour cream.

Step 3: Once toasted, the almonds were not used. Add them to the platter with the other salad ingredients.

Step 3: Arrange the salad on a platter, not on a baking sheet.

Chickpeas with Spinach and Feta

Yield: This recipe serves 4 people, not 1 person.

Ingredients: The scallions can't be left whole; they need to be thinly sliced.

Ingredients: You can't really thinly shave feta; it should be crumbled.

Step 1: 200°F is too low for baking. 400°F is the correct temperature.

Step 1: You're using olive oil, not peanut oil.

Step 2: The spinach should be cooked in a skillet, not on a grill.

Step 2: To stop the cooking, rinse the spinach under cold water.

Step 3: There are 3 tablespoons of olive oil remaining, not 1 tablespoon.

Step 3: Season with salt, too, not just pepper.

Step 3: There are no nuts in the recipe; scatter the cheese on top before baking.

Garlicky Roasted Haricots Verts

Yield: This recipe serves 6 people, not 16.

Ingredients: You're making haricots verts, not lima beans.

Ingredients: The recipe should call for 1 tablespoon of minced thyme, not 10 tablespoons.

Ingredients: You're using freshly ground black pepper, not bell pepper.

Step 1: The garlic has been left out of the recipe. Add it to the beans with the olive oil and thyme.

Step 1: The beans are haricots verts, not rouges.

Step 1: The haricots verts should be spread in a roasting pan (the recipe doesn't say what cooking vessel to use).

Step 2: There are no thyme sprigs to discard because the thyme is already minced.

Step 2: You're using lemon juice, not lime juice.

Step 2: Serve the dish warm.

Sweet Corn Soup with Tomatoes

Ingredients: The scallion parts are white, not yellow.

Ingredients: You should be using basil leaves, not stems.

Step 1: Combine ¼ cup each of the corn and tomatoes, not potatoes.

Step 1: Set aside in a cool place, not a warm one.

Step 2: Heat the olive oil over moderately low heat; high heat will burn the scallions.

Step 2: The word "stock" is missing after "chicken."

Step 3: Strain the soup through a fine-mesh sieve, not a kitchen towel.

Step 3: The cream should not be whipped.

Step 4: Refrigerate the soup for at least 3 hours; 12 hours is longer than necessary for chilling.

Step 4: The small basil leaves have been left out of the recipe. Use them for garnish after topping the soup with the reserved corn and tomatoes.

Navy Bean Soup

Ingredients: The beans should be soaked overnight, not roasted.

Ingredients: The celery should be thinly sliced like the carrots and onion.

Ingredients: 5 bay leaves is too much; the recipe should call for 2 leaves.

Step 1: The chicken stock has been omitted from the recipe. Add it to the pot with the water.

Step 1: The ham isn't shredded at this point—it's still on the hocks.

Step 1: Bring to a boil over high heat, not low.

Step 1: Simmer until the beans are tender, not tough.

Step 2: The shredded ham was never used. Stir it into the pot with the pureed soup.

Step 2: Too much seasoning with salt and pepper!

Step 2: Drizzle with olive oil, not avocado oil.

Herbed Cheese Crackers

Ingredients: The recipe should call for 1 teaspoon of chopped fresh rosemary, not whole sprigs.

Ingredients: 3 sticks of butter is far too much; the correct amount is 3 tablespoons.

Step 1: Don't puree the dry ingredients, just pulse them.

Step 1: You're using black pepper, not red.

Step 1: Rosemary and thyme are herbs, not spices.

Step 1: The butter is cold, not melted.

Step 1: Don't pulse for 5 minutes or you will have some pretty tough crackers. Pulse just until a dough forms, about 1 minute.

Step 1: Don't press the dough into a log, simply roll it.

Step 2: 90 minutes of baking will burn these crackers to a crisp; 30 minutes is the correct time.

Step 2: The crackers will need to cool to crisp up, so they shouldn't be served hot. Transfer them to a rack to cool before serving.

Eggplant Caponata

Ingredients: A mini eggplant will be too small. Use a standard one.

Ingredients: The onion should be finely chopped like the celery and garlic.

Ingredients: There is no reason to use confectioners' sugar in this savory recipe; it should be granulated sugar.

Ingredients: The basil should be fresh, not dried.

Step 1: The colander doesn't need to be set in cheesecloth. Just place it in the sink or in another bowl to catch any liquid from the eggplant.

Step 1: 1 cup of kosher salt is too much; 1 tablespoon is the correct amount.

Step 2: A large skillet is too big; a small one is right for toasting the pine nuts.

Step 3: The garlic has been left out of the recipe.

Add it to the skillet with the drained eggplant, onion and celery.

Step 3: It will take more than 2 minutes for the vegetables to get soft and golden brown—more like 15 minutes.

Step 3: After they were toasted, the pine nuts were not used in the dish. Sprinkle them on the caponata before serving.

Summer Panzanella

Ingredients: The shallot should be minced, not left whole.

Ingredients: The bread is called ciabatta; cioppino is a type of seafood stew.

Ingredients: Dry out the bread in the oven, not the fridge.

Ingredients: It should say "½ cup" not "½ basil."

Step 1: The tomatoes have accumulated juices, not sauce.

Step 1: Place the tomatoes in a colander, not a cup.

Step 2: You're using red wine vinegar, not red wine.

Step 2: After they were seasoned and drained, the tomatoes never got used in the salad. Stir them in with the bread and cucumbers.

Step 2: There is no celery in the recipe.

Step 2: The basil has been omitted from the recipe. Stir it into the salad with the mozzarella just before serving.

Tomato, Feta and Kale Frittata

Ingredients: A turnip is not interchangeable with an onion. Don't use a turnip here.

Ingredients: You're using cherry or grape tomatoes, not cherries or grapes.

Ingredients: The milk should not be curdled.

Ingredients: Dill sprigs, not leaves, are what you want for garnish here.

Step 1: The onion and garlic will burn in 25 minutes; the correct cooking time is about 5 minutes.

Step 1: Add the kale in batches, letting each batch wilt before you add the next.

Step 2: The pan should be greased with olive oil, not butter.

Step 2: The correct pan size is 9 by 13 inches (there is no such pan that's 15 by 23 inches).

Step 2: There's no sour cream in the recipe; the eggs are whisked with milk.

Step 2: It's a frittata mixture, not an omelet mixture.

Shakshuka

Ingredients: 1 cup of olive oil is far too much; 1 tablespoon is the correct amount.

Ingredients: The cumin is ground, so there are no whole seeds.

Ingredients: Pimentón is smoked paprika; paprikash is a traditional Hungarian stew.

Step 1: The feta cheese doesn't get sautéed with the onion and bell pepper. It's sprinkled over the eggs and sauce at the end of Step 2.

Step 1: There is no cinnamon in the recipe.

Step 1: Simmer the sauce until it is slightly thickened, not until a paste forms.

Step 2: Use a large spoon, not a glass, to make the wells in the sauce.

Step 2: Make 6 wells in the sauce for the 6 eggs.

Step 2: Cook until the egg whites are firm (the yolks should be a little runny, though).

Step 2: Garnish with parsley, not cilantro.

Bonnie's Hot Blue Crab Dip

Ingredients: At 3 inches, the baguette slices are too thick. Make them ½ inch thick.

Ingredients: The ingredient list should specify what kind of oil is used—extra-virgin olive oil.

Ingredients: This recipe is for blue crab, not imitation crabmeat. Use 1 pound lump or jumbo lump crab.

Step 1: The baguette slices should be toasted on a baking sheet, not in a pie plate.

Step 2: The Worcestershire sauce has been left out of the recipe. Add it to the large bowl with the cream cheese mixture.

Step 2: The Old Bay has also been left out of the recipe, and also should be added with the cream cheese mixture.

Step 2: You don't want to vigorously stir in the crab or it will break apart too much; gently fold it in to retain the lumps.

Step 2: 5 minutes is not enough time to bake the dip. The correct baking time is about 25 minutes.

Step 2: Serve the dip while it's hot, not chilled.

Step 2: This is a crab dip, not a sauce.

Grilled Shrimp with Greek Salad

Ingredients: Peeling and shelling are the same thing. The shrimp needs to be peeled and deveined.

Ingredients: The feta is Greek, not Asian.

Step 1: The bowl should be nonreactive—glass, ceramic or stainless steel, for example—not reactive. A bowl made out of aluminum, say, will react with the citrus in the marinade and may affect its flavor.

Step 1: You're using lemon juice, not lime juice.

Step 1: There is no black pepper in the recipe.

Step 2: You're using bell peppers, not chile peppers.

Step 2: There are 2 teaspoons of oregano remaining, not 2 tablespoons.

Step 3: Preheat a grill pan, not a sauté pan.

Step 3: It's feta cheese, not Muenster.

Step 3: The shrimp needs to be plated, too; make sure to add it to the salad before serving.

Shrimp and Kimchi Quesadillas

Ingredients: Hazelnut oil won't taste good here. Just use vegetable oil.

Ingredients: Bacon kimchi? That isn't a thing, though it sounds good. Standard kimchi is fine.

Ingredients: They don't make 16-inch corn tortillas. Use 6-inch ones.

Step 1: 12 to 13 minutes is too long to boil the shrimp; the correct cooking time is 2 to 3 minutes.

Step 2: The oven is preheating to keep the quesadillas warm, not to cook them. 250°F is ample heat for that.

Step 3: The amount of cheese used doesn't match the amount in the ingredient list. Each quesadilla should get 2 tablespoons of cheese on the bottom and another 2 tablespoons on top, for a total of ¼ cup of cheese per quesadilla.

Step 3: You have to put the second tortilla on the quesadilla before pressing it.

Step 3: Make sure the serving platter is heatproof before putting it in the oven.

Step 3: These are not enchiladas.

Step 4: The sour cream has been omitted from the recipe. Serve it with the finished quesadillas, along with the sliced scallions.

Grilled Scallop Skewers with Serrano Salsa

Ingredients: 10 large shallots is far too many; 5 large shallots is the correct amount.

Ingredients: The recipe title says "Serrano Salsa," so the ingredient list should call for serrano chiles, not habaneros.

Step 1: A very small skillet won't work here; use a medium one.

Step 1: Scrape the shallots into a medium bowl, not onto a plate.

Step 1: The serrano chiles are finely chopped, not thinly sliced.

Step 2: There is only 1 tablespoon of minced garlic remaining, not 3.

Step 2: There are 2 tablespoons of lime juice remaining, not 1.

Step 2: Aluminum will react with the acidic marinade, and may affect its flavor; use a nonreactive dish, such as glass, ceramic or stainless steel.

Step 2: If you refrigerate the scallops overnight, the acid in the citrus juice will cook them. The correct marinating time is about 30 minutes.

Step 3: Grill the scallops for 3 minutes per side, not 30.

Lobster Rolls

Ingredients: The lobsters should be live, not cooked.

Ingredients: The lobster salad is not made with vegetable shortening; use mayonnaise.

Step 1: You'll need a very large pot to cook the lobsters.

Step 1: Cook the lobsters until they are bright red.

Step 2: The lobsters should be cool when you handle them, not very hot.

Step 2: Don't forget to include the claw meat in the lobster rolls.

Step 3: Season with a pinch of cayenne, not a handful. (Ouch!)

Step 3: The lobster should be chilled when it's folded with the mayonnaise, not hot.

Step 3: The chives have been left out of the recipe. Add them to the lobster salad along with the celery.

Step 4: You're using split hot dog buns, not bagels.

Cioppino

Ingredients: 5 teaspoons of crushed red pepper is too much; ½ teaspoon is the correct amount.

Ingredients: Salmon is not a firm white fish; don't use it here.

Ingredients: It's king crab leg, not thigh.

Step 1: A 1-quart pot is not large; you'll need an 8-quart pot for this recipe.

Step 1: There are no carrots in the recipe.

Step 1: The shrimp should not be added in Step 1 or it will be terribly overcooked. It's added toward the end of cooking in Step 2.

Step 1: You're using chicken stock or low-sodium broth, not vegetable stock.

Step 2: Spoon the stew into bowls.

Step 2: There's no rosemary in the recipe; garnish with basil and parsley.

Step 2: Crusty bread is way better than pita for sopping up all that delicious broth.

Summer Cod Bake

Yield: This recipe serves 4 people, not 12.

Ingredients: The onion should be thinly sliced.

Ingredients: Panko are Japanese breadcrumbs, not Swedish.

Ingredients: Pecorino isn't cream cheese.

Ingredients: The recipe is for cod, not salmon.

Step 1: The baking dish should be glass or ceramic, not plastic.

Step 1: The zucchini has been omitted from the recipe. Add it to the baking dish with the peppers, tomatoes and onion.

Step 1: You're roasting the vegetables, not simmering them.

Step 2: The panko is combined with pecorino cheese and basil; there's no butter in the recipe.

Step 2: 1 hour of roasting will overcook the fish; the correct time is about 15 minutes.

Roasted Salmon with Avocado Chimichurri

Ingredients: There's no need to mince the garlic since it's going into the food processor. Just peel the cloves and throw them in whole.

Ingredients: You want the oregano leaves, not the stems.

Ingredients: 2 tablespoons of crushed red pepper will be *very* spicy. The correct amount is 2 teaspoons.

Ingredients: You're using red wine vinegar, not red wine rice vinegar.

Ingredients: You need to halve the avocados first, then you can pit and dice them.

Step 1: You're using garlic cloves, not heads.

Step 1: It's not necessary to stir constantly for the flavors to come together.

Step 2: You will have very overcooked salmon after 40 minutes. The correct cooking time is about 12 minutes.

Step 3: There is no jicama in the recipe.

Step 3: Serve the salmon on plates, not saucers.

Miso Cod with Edamame Salad

Ingredients: Mirin and dry white wine are not interchangeable; don't use white wine.

Ingredients: Delicate flounder isn't as meaty as black cod or salmon. It wouldn't hold up well in this dish.

Ingredients: You're making an edamame salad, not a slaw.

Ingredients: The edamame should be shelled, not in the pods.

Ingredients: 2¼ cups of cilantro is too much; the correct amount is ¼ cup.

Step 1: They are cod fillets, not breasts.

Step 2: The grated ginger has been left out of the edamame salad. Whisk it into the large bowl with the canola oil, rice vinegar and sesame oil.

Step 2: There is no olive oil in the recipe; it should be sesame oil.

Step 3: At 500°F, the oven temperature is too high. The correct temperature is 425°F.

Step 3: The scallion is thinly sliced, not minced.

Chilean Sea Bass with Crispy Chorizo Crumbs and Potatoes

Ingredients: Panko are Japanese breadcrumbs, not Chinese.

Ingredients: It's extra-virgin olive oil, not canola.

Ingredients: Chilean sea bass is the correct name, not Chilean striped bass.

Step 1: The recipe doesn't say what temperature to preheat the oven to (425°F).

Step 1: You want to cook the chorizo in a skillet, not a grill pan.

Step 2: You've already added the cheese to the chorizo crumbs in Step 1; it's not used here, too.

Step 2: The potatoes won't start to soften and turn golden in just 5 minutes; the correct time is about 15 minutes.

Step 2: There is no shrimp in the recipe; this should say "Season the fish fillets."

Step 2: There is no cayenne in the recipe; season the fish with salt and black pepper.

Step 2: The olives have been left out of the recipe. Scatter them over the fish before serving.

Baked Chicken Parmigiana

Ingredients: Use olive oil or another savory cooking spray, not baking spray.

Ingredients: Chicken cutlets don't have bones.

Ingredients: To measure ¼ cup of Parmesan, you

need to grate it first. This should call for ¼ cup freshly grated Parmesan cheese.

Step 1: You're spreading tomato sauce, not pesto.

Step 1: Put the eggs and breadcrumbs in two separate shallow bowls.

Step 2: Dip the cutlets in the eggs; there is no milk in the recipe.

Step 2: The skillet needs to be hot for cooking the cutlets.

Step 2: 30 minutes is way too long to brown the bottom of the cutlets; the correct time is about 3 minutes.

Step 2: 20 minutes is too long to brown the other side of the cutlets; the correct time is about 2 minutes.

Step 3: Sprinkle the cutlets with Parmesan cheese, not cheddar.

Crisp Roasted Chicken Breasts with Cucumber Salad

Ingredients: You're using chicken breasts, not drumsticks.

Ingredients: They aren't parsley flowers, they're parsley leaves.

Ingredients: It's extra-virgin olive oil, not caper oil.

Step 1: It's not duck, it's chicken.

Step 1: Roast the chicken on a baking sheet, not a pie plate.

Step 2: You don't need a large skillet to toast 1 teaspoon of seeds; a small one will do.

Step 2: You're using cumin seeds, not coriander.

Step 3: Toss the salad, don't puree it.

Step 3: The scallions aren't grilled.

Step 3: After they were toasted, the cumin seeds were not used. Toss them with the rest of the salad ingredients.

Spicy Cilantro-Roasted Chicken

Ingredients: The jalapeño seeds give heat, not sweetness.

Ingredients: The chicken should be cut into 6 pieces, not 16.

Ingredients: The mint should be fresh, not dried.

Step 2: You're using coriander seeds, not cumin.

Step 2: Marinate the chicken in a resealable plastic bag.

Step 2: Don't leave the chicken to marinate at room temperature; keep it in the fridge.

Step 3: There is only 1 tablespoon of lemon juice remaining, not 3 tablespoons.

Step 3: You've just made a sauce, not a salad.

Step 3: You are roasting the chicken, not steaming it.

Step 4: Arrange the chicken pieces in a roasting pan, not a Bundt pan.

Honey-Roasted Chicken with New Potatoes

Ingredients: Small young potatoes are called "new potatoes"; don't look for "old potatoes."

Ingredients: The chicken should be 4½ to 5 pounds.

Ingredients: Ground fennel is simply fennel seed that's been ground; it isn't fresh.

Step 1: You'll need a roasting pan, not a pie plate.

Step 1: Arrange the chicken pieces on top of the potatoes, not under them.

Step 1: You're using shallots; there are no scallions in the recipe.

Step 2: It's not honey-mustard; it's honey and mustard.

Step 2: The remaining 1 tablespoon of olive oil has been omitted from the recipe. Stir it into the honey and mustard mixture along with the ground fennel and minced thyme.

Step 2: Brush the honey and mustard mixture over the chicken, not the potatoes.

Step 2: This dish serves 4 people, so it should be served on 4 plates.

Chicken, Sausage and White Bean Stew

Ingredients: It should say 2 medium "garlic cloves," not "garlics."

Ingredients: The recipe uses boneless, skinless chicken thighs, not wings.

Ingredients: 8 cups of stock is 64 ounces, and that's what you need for this recipe.

Ingredients: Thyme comes in sprigs, not stalks.

Step 1: A large pot is the correct cooking vessel for this stew.

Step 2: "Step 4" is actually Step 2.

Step 2: The recipe calls for white beans, not kidney beans.

Step 2: Cook the barley until it's tender.

Step 2: When you discard the thyme sprigs, pick out the bay leaves, too.

Step 2: Serve the stew in wide, shallow bowls.

Easy Chicken Piccata

Ingredients: Use all-purpose flour, not cake flour.

Ingredients: 8 thin chicken cutlets should weigh about 1½ pounds total, not 5 pounds.

Ingredients: If you want to prepare the piccata with wine instead of stock, a dry white wine is preferable to a fruity red.

Ingredients: The capers you want are bottled in brine (salted capers don't need to be drained).

Step 2: The chicken is pan-fried, not deep-fried.

Step 2: The chicken will cook through and turn golden after about 3 minutes per side; 10 minutes per side will burn it.

Step 2: Transfer the second batch of chicken to the platter with the first batch.

Step 3: The yummy bits to be scraped up will be browned, not white.

Step 3: Don't scrape with a metal spatula! Use a wooden spoon.

Step 3: You're using lemon juice, not orange juice.

Pork Tenderloin Medallions with Mustard Sauce

Ingredients: Cut the pork into slices or medallions, not strips.

Ingredients: ¼ cup of cumin is way too much! The correct amount is 2 teaspoons.

Ingredients: 3 bunches of thyme is also too much. (A bunch of thyme can include anywhere from a few sprigs to dozens.) The correct amount is 3 sprigs.

Ingredients: Use flat-leaf parsley for garnish, not beet greens.

Step 1: You don't season the pork with sugar.

Step 1: The pork needs to cook for only 3 minutes per side, and you don't want it well done or it will be very tough and dry.

Step 2: There is no coriander in the recipe.

Step 2: You're adding wine, not vinegar.

Step 2: It should say to add the "chicken stock," not "chicken bones."

Step 2: Discard the thyme sprigs before serving.

Pork Stew with Escarole

Ingredients: The alternative to fresh rosemary should be regular dried rosemary, not freeze-dried.

Ingredients: The potatoes should be cut into 1-inch chunks, not 10-inch chunks.

Ingredients: The chicken broth should be low in sodium, not high.

Ingredients: According to the recipe title, you're using escarole, not butter lettuce.
Step 1: 20 minutes is too long to brown the pork. The correct time is about 2 minutes per side.
Step 2: There is only 1 tablespoon of olive oil remaining, not 3.
Step 2: You're using white wine, not red.
Step 2: The onions are already in the pot.
Step 2: The potatoes should be tender, not firm.
Step 3: Serve the stew hot, not chilled.

Lamb Kebabs with Tzatziki

Yield: The recipe serves 4 people, not 12.
Ingredients: You're using lamb shoulder, not skin.
Ingredients: Make the tzatziki with plain Greek yogurt; vanilla would be pretty bad here.
Ingredients: The garlic is grated on a Microplane zester, not a microwave.
Step 1: You're making a marinade, not a dressing.
Step 1: You're not pureeing the marinade ingredients, just whisking them together.
Step 1: Marinate the lamb at most overnight, not for 2 weeks!
Step 3: There is no mint in the recipe—though you could add some!
Step 3: You're grilling lamb, not pork.
Step 4: Thread the lamb onto skewers, not forks.

Braised Lamb Shanks with Gremolata

Ingredients: The lamb shanks are about 1 pound each, not 1 ounce.
Ingredients: You'll need 6 large carrots for this recipe, not 6 baby carrots.
Ingredients: The tomatoes are canned in puree, not soup.
Ingredients: It's a can of chicken broth, not consommé.

Step 1: Season the shanks with salt and pepper before browning them.
Step 1: A small plate won't hold all the shanks; use a very large one.
Step 2: The celery has been left out of the recipe. Add it to the casserole with the onions and carrots.
Step 2: Be sure to cover the pot when you braise in the oven.
Step 3: The gremolata is made with lemon zest here, not orange.
Step 4: Simmer the liquid in the casserole over high heat, not very low.

Grilled Hanger Steak Sandwiches with Scallion-Wasabi Mayo

Yield: The recipe makes 4 sandwiches, not 8.
Ingredients: The scallion needs to be finely chopped; use the white and light green parts only.
Step 1: You'll need a large bowl to hold the steak and marinade.
Step 1: The orange juice has been left out of the recipe. Whisk it into the marinade with the other citrus juice and zests.
Step 2: You're using wasabi powder, not paste (you're forming a paste, however).
Step 3: Remove from the marinade, not from the soup.
Step 3: 15 to 20 minutes is too long to grill the steak. Grill it for 4 to 5 minutes per side for medium-rare meat.
Step 4: It's a scallion-wasabi mayonnaise, not shallot-wasabi.
Step 4: You're using ciabatta rolls, not hot dog buns.
Step 4: Thinly slice the steak across the grain, not with it.

Flank Steak Salad with Pecorino and Radishes

Ingredients: The recipe should specify what kind of oil to use—extra-virgin olive oil.

Ingredients: You're using plain honey, not honey molasses.

Ingredients: The garlic needs to be minced so it can be used in the dressing.

Ingredients: This is a recipe for flank steak, not rib eye.

Ingredients: The romaine should be coarsely chopped, not left whole.

Ingredients: You're using the arugula leaves, too, not just the stems.

Step 1: The recipe calls for lime juice, not lemon.

Step 2: There are 4 tablespoons of olive oil left, not 2; use all 4 remaining tablespoons in the dressing.

Step 3: 1 hour is too long for the steak to rest. Let it rest for just 10 minutes before slicing.

Step 4: There is no spinach in the recipe; it should be arugula.

Beer-Braised Beef Short Ribs

Ingredients: The ribs shouldn't be cut so small; make them 2-inch pieces.

Ingredients: 3 cups of beer equals 24 ounces—that's what's needed here.

Ingredients: Pale lager is not a dark beer.

Step 1: Don't forget to brown the remaining ribs.

Step 2: The garlic is finely chopped, not sliced.

Step 2: Cook the flour and tomato paste for about 2 minutes before adding the beer. This eliminates some of the raw flour taste.

Step 2: The brown sugar has been omitted from the recipe. Add it to the pot with the beef stock, thyme sprigs and bay leaf.

Step 3: Cover the pot with an ovenproof lid, not plastic wrap.

Step 3: The oven was never preheated. It should be at 350°F.

Step 3: Before serving, discard the thyme sprigs and bay leaf.

Cavatappi with Italian Sausage and Spinach

Ingredients: You're using kosher salt, not pretzel salt.

Ingredients: 4 teaspoons of crushed red pepper will be way too spicy. The correct amount is ¼ teaspoon.

Ingredients: The cheese isn't for snacking; it's for sprinkling on the pasta.

Step 1: You're boiling the cavatappi, not sautéing it.

Step 2: You're using a red onion, not green onions.

Step 2: 25 minutes is too long to soften the onion. The correct time is about 5 minutes.

Step 2: Break up the meat with a wooden spoon, not a knife—bad idea in a skillet!

Step 2: The spinach has been left out of the recipe. Add it to the skillet with the tomatoes.

Step 2: 3 seconds isn't enough time to soften the tomatoes. The correct time is about 3 minutes.

Step 3: Stir the cavatappi and cooking water into the skillet, not the bowl.

Pasta Bolognese

Ingredients: "Pancetta" is the correct spelling.

Ingredients: ¼ pound of penne is not enough for 8 people; you'll need 1½ pounds.

Step 1: If you cook the vegetables and pancetta over high heat, they'll burn. Cook over moderately low heat.

Step 1: 45 minutes is too long to soften the vegetables. The correct time is about 12 minutes.

Step 2: There are 3 tablespoons of olive oil left, not 2; use all 3 remaining tablespoons to cook the meat.

Step 2: There are no leeks in the recipe.

Step 2: The ingredient list calls for white wine, not red.

Step 2: You can't bring the sauce to a quick boil over very low heat; it should be over high heat.

Step 3: The ingredient list calls for penne, not spaghetti.

Step 3: The Parmesan cheese has been left out of the recipe. Serve it with the finished pasta.

Baked Ziti

Ingredients: You can't make this with angel hair pasta, but penne would be a good alternative to ziti.

Ingredients: You're using Italian sausage, not breakfast sausage.

Ingredients: 8 cups of ricotta is far too much. The correct amount is 8 ounces, or 1 cup.

Ingredients: Camembert cheese won't work here (especially not shredded!), but mozzarella will.

Step 1: You're boiling the ziti here, not baking it.

Step 2: You're using an onion, not a shallot.

Step 2: Break up the sausage with a wooden spoon or a spatula, not chopsticks.

Step 2: It's crushed red pepper, not pink.

Step 4: 5 minutes is not long enough to bake the ziti. The correct time is about 30 minutes.

Step 4: Don't refrigerate the baked ziti; just let it stand at room temp for 15 minutes before serving.

Penne with Spring Vegetables

Ingredients: 4 heads of garlic is too much. The correct amount is 4 medium garlic cloves.

Ingredients: Snap peas aren't really deveined; just remove the strings.

Ingredients: You don't really need to stem a zucchini.

Ingredients: The cherry tomatoes can be halved any which way!

Ingredients: Dried figs don't belong in this recipe.

Step 1: Cook the penne until it's al dente, not very soft.

Step 2: 20 minutes is too long to soften the shallot and garlic. The correct time is about 3 minutes.

Step 2: The zucchini has been omitted from the recipe. Add it to the skillet with the snap peas and asparagus.

Step 2: You're cooking vegetables, not fruit.

Step 3: There is no reserved pasta sauce. You're adding reserved pasta cooking water.

Fettuccine with Mushrooms

Ingredients: Delicata is a type of winter squash, not a mushroom.

Ingredients: ½ cup of thyme is far too much. The correct amount is 1 tablespoon.

Ingredients: ¼ pound of fettuccine won't be enough for 8 people. The correct amount is 2 pounds.

Ingredients: Fettuccine is not a short noodle, so this should say "or a similar long noodle of your choice."

Ingredients: The parsley is for sprinkling, not dusting.

Step 1: To soften the garlic and shallots, the heat shouldn't be so high! Moderately low heat is best here.

Step 2: You're using red wine, not red wine vinegar.

Step 3: "Step 2" is repeated. The second "Step 2" is actually Step 3.

Step 3: The serving bowl should be large, not small.

Step 3: Don't forget to use the rest of the mushroom sauce. Spoon it over the pasta before sprinkling with the parsley.

Rich and Creamy Potato Gratin

Ingredients: The additional butter is for greasing the baking dish, not a baking sheet.

Ingredients: The potatoes should be peeled and thinly sliced (not thinly peeled).

Ingredients: Heavy cream is by definition not fat-free.

Step 1: Grease the inside of the baking dish, not the outside.

Step 1: Grease the baking dish with butter, not oil.

Step 1: The herbs are fresh, not dried.

Step 1: The layering should be repeated twice more, not three times.

Step 2: The Gruyère cheese has been left out of the recipe. Sprinkle it over the potatoes before putting the gratin in the oven.

Step 2: 15 minutes is not enough time to bake the gratin. It will need about an hour.

Step 2: You're baking potatoes, not tomatoes.

Cinnamon Sugar Cookies

Ingredients: Use a standard chicken egg, not a goose egg.

Ingredients: It's not chocolate extract, but vanilla.

Step 1: You don't need to use a very large bowl for sifting the dry ingredients—a medium one will do.

Step 1: There is no baking powder in the recipe.

Step 1: The first sugar used (¼ cup) is granulated, not confectioners'.

Step 1: The dough should be refrigerated until firm, not soft.

Step 2: There is ½ cup of granulated sugar remaining, not 2 cups.

Step 2: Spread the cinnamon sugar on a plate or in a wide, shallow bowl.

Step 3: At 3 inches, these cookies will be far too thick. The correct thickness is ⅓ inch.

Step 3: Bake the cookies until they are golden, not dark brown.

Almond Shortbread Squares

Yield: This recipe makes only 60 shortbread squares, not, sadly, 600.

Ingredients: You are using flour, not flower.

Ingredients: The word "large" is repeated before "egg yolk."

Ingredients: ½ teaspoon of almonds is not nearly enough. The correct amount is 1 cup.

Step 1: 125°F is too low to bake the shortbread. The correct temperature is 325°F.

Step 1: You're using the bowl of a standing mixer, not the plate.

Step 1: You're using kosher salt, not Himalayan.

Step 2: "Step 3" is actually Step 2.

Step 2: Press the almonds into the dough with the palm of your hand, not the back.

Step 2: You've made shortbread, not meringues.

Lemon-Coconut Bars

Yield: They're not cookies, they're bars.

Ingredients: The crust should be made with confectioners' sugar, not raw sugar.

Ingredients: You should be using 1½ tablespoons of finely grated lemon zest, not strips of peel.

Ingredients: 4 tablespoons is far too much baking powder. The correct amount is 2 teaspoons.

Ingredients: You're using pure vanilla extract, not a bean.

Step 1: Process the dough for only a few seconds, just until it comes together (otherwise it will be very tough).

Step 1: The recipe doesn't say to turn the oven on. Preheat it to 350°F before you start making the crust.

Step 2: You'll need a large bowl for the filling, not a small one.

Step 2: Don't forget to use the remaining coconut. Sprinkle it over the filling before baking.

Step 2: The yield is 24 bars, not 48.

Hazelnut Fudge Brownies

Ingredients: Use a neutral nonstick cooking spray, or a baking spray, not olive oil spray.

Ingredients: 2 tablespoons is far too much baking powder. The correct amount is ½ teaspoon.

Ingredients: There is no need for the chocolate to be frozen.

Step 1: You've toasted hazelnuts, not pecans.

Step 1: Use a clean kitchen towel, not a used one. (Gross!)

Step 2: You don't need to spray the baking pan heavily. Just a light spray will do.

Step 2: You can combine the dry ingredients in a medium bowl instead of a very large one.

Step 2: To melt the butter and chocolate, the pot of water should be simmering.

Step 3: Don't forget to add the cooled chocolate-butter mixture to the batter. Beat it in with the hazelnut liqueur .

Step 4: Let the brownies cool before slicing and serving—if you can wait that long!

Almond Butter–Chocolate Chip Bars

Ingredients: There are two types of sugar used in these bars—the recipe should specify each kind. The first one in the ingredient list (½ cup) is granulated sugar; the second one (½ cup plus 2 tablespoons) should be light brown sugar.

Ingredients: It's pure vanilla extract, not seeds.

Step 1: 550°F is too hot to bake the bars. The correct temperature is 350°F.

Step 1: The correct pan size is 9 by 9 inches (there is no 8-by-11-inch pan).

Step 2: You should whisk the flour with the baking powder and salt, not dredge it.

Step 2: You're using almond butter, not peanut butter—though that would work well, too!

Step 2: A rubber spatula is a much better tool than a fork for scraping down the bowl.

Step 2: The chocolate chips have been omitted from the recipe. Add them to the batter after the dry ingredients are incorporated.

Step 3: Rotate the pan halfway through baking, not after only 5 minutes.

Step 3: Cut the bars, don't crumble them.

Chocolate Chip Pumpkin Bread

Yield: It's a loaf, not a pie.

Ingredients: The cinnamon should be ground.

Ingredients: The eggs should not be hard-cooked.

Step 1: Dust the loaf pan with flour, not kosher salt.

Step 2: You'll need a large bowl for whisking the dry ingredients.

Step 2: The granulated sugar has been left out of the recipe. Whisk it with the other dry ingredients.

Step 3: The chocolate chips have also been left out of the recipe. Stir them into the batter once the wet and dry ingredients are combined.

Step 3: Pour the batter into the prepared loaf pan, not a skillet.

Step 3: The skewer shouldn't be wet; it should come out with just a few moist crumbs attached.

Step 4: A rack is the best tool for cooling the loaf.

Warm Blackberry Custard

Ingredients: You need unsalted butter to grease the baking dish for this sweet custard, not olive oil.

Ingredients: Flour is called for twice in the ingredient list. The first quantity mentioned (⅓ cup plus 2 tablespoons) should actually be for granulated sugar.

Ingredients: There are no chives in this recipe. (Yuck.)

Step 1: Whisk the eggs, sugar, vanilla and lemon zest until light and pale, not very stiff.

Step 1: You're using heavy cream, not skim milk.

Step 1: It's custard, not cake batter.

Step 1: The recipe never says to preheat the oven. Preheat it to 325°F when you grease the baking dish.

Step 2: The recipe calls for blackberries, not blueberries.

Step 2: 5 minutes isn't long enough to bake the custard. The correct time is about 45 minutes.

Step 2: Serve the custard warm (or at room temperature), not frozen.

Strawberry-Rhubarb Crisp

Ingredients: You'll need cold diced butter for the crisp topping, not melted butter.

Ingredients: 1½ stalks is not enough rhubarb. The correct amount is 1½ pounds of rhubarb.

Ingredients: The recipe should specify that the second sugar listed (1 cup) is granulated (the dark brown sugar is for the crisp topping).

Step 1: You're using dark brown sugar, not light brown.

Step 1: There is no need to vigorously mix the ingredients here.

Step 2: The strawberries are sliced, not whole.

Step 2: The remaining 3 tablespoons of flour have been omitted from the recipe. Toss with the fruit filling.

Step 2: You're using orange zest and juice, not lemon (though you could swap in lemon if you like).

Step 2: The recipe never says to preheat the oven. It should be preheated to 350°F at the beginning of Step 1.

Step 2: The baked crisp topping should be golden brown, not pale.

Peach Galette

Yield: The directions in Step 3 will create a galette that's smaller than 12 inches. It will be more like 8 inches.

Ingredients: "Grated" is misspelled.

Ingredients: You should use distilled white vinegar to make the dough (it helps tenderize it), not red wine vinegar.

Ingredients: Halved peaches will be too big. Slice them about ½ inch thick.

Step 1: You're making galette dough, not cookie dough.

Step 2: You'll need a medium bowl for making the filling.

Step 2: The cornstarch has been left out of the recipe. Toss it with the rest of the filling ingredients.

Step 3: The recipe should tell you to use a baking sheet with a rim, or the juices from the galette will likely run over into your oven.

Step 4: The oven is preheating too late. Preheat it at the beginning of Step 3.

Step 4: The egg wash and coarse sugar have been left out of the recipe. Before baking the galette, brush the edge of the dough with the egg wash and sprinkle generously with coarse sugar.

Apple Crumble Pie

Ingredients: You're using vegetable shortening, not vegetarian shortening.

Step 1: Make the crust in a food processor, not a large skillet.

Step 2: There are no pears in this apple crumble pie.

Step 2: Toss the filling to combine, not until it's warm.

Step 3: The pie plate should be 9 inches, not 12.

Step 3: The apple filling is never added to the pie. Mound it on the dough before sprinkling the topping over it.

Step 4: You're making the topping, not a frosting.

Step 4: The ingredient list calls for dark brown sugar, not light brown.

Step 5: 10 minutes isn't long enough to bake the pie. The correct baking time is about 40 minutes.

Step 5: The crust shouldn't be bubbling, but the filling should be.

Maple Walnut Pie

Yield: The pie will be 9 inches, not 12.

Ingredients: You need ice water for the pie crust, not hot water.

Step 1: You're making the crust here, not a cake.

Step 1: Pulse the pie dough just until it starts to come together, not until it's thoroughly blended (or it will be very tough).

Step 1: Refrigerate the dough for at least 30 minutes, not 3 minutes.

Step 2: The nuts won't toast in 5 minutes at 200°F. The oven temperature should be 400°F.

Step 3: Don't roll the dough with a damp rolling pin! It should be lightly floured.

Step 3: The overhanging dough will be about 1 inch, not 6 inches.

Step 4: The maple syrup has been left out of the recipe. Whisk it with the eggs, sugar, melted butter, vanilla and salt.

Step 4: The ingredient list says to serve with whipped cream, not ice cream (though either would be delicious).

WORD SEARCHES

The Fish Counter

```
B O N I Z N A R B M X S A S F
O A D S C B S U A G S L N B P
R M R E M H I C X C W E C A Y
N E H R R A K N H X O S H R V
S H D I A E L H Z U R S O C V
Q E M N R M S C B J D U V U L
Y P M E U N P B B F M Y N R
Q B L L H O O N Z L I C E S B
N O M L A S L C D G S V R O A
L O B S T E R F T I H E E N G
Z W G Q N M X C Z O T C U K Z
S Y A Y J L N S M S P T D H X
P X Y N I E D J Y W R U R V Q
J W U I L A D O D Y J A S Z C
A U M L N X U Y C G T G T R L
```

For the Sweet Tooth

```
S B T E Z C E T D Y C X S N S
T S R Q U C O A U U E N J A Y
D O N O L G E B P H I S H D K
Z Z O A W R N C B F M G D A B
Z S I O B N A I F L X N A N L
U R S N D K I U R W E C E I O
C V R P E D M E W E X R R S N
L O Z S G J E I S U M P B H D
C C U S I M A R I T X U T S I
P Q B O B A S C F Z Y J R E E
D O U G H N U T S I F S O I S
T E P U D D I N G K M P H K Z
T X S E Z B T P G Y M E S O R
R B C F Z N C K C H G M S O Q
Z W A Y H I O Z N U A E N C I
```

Chefs of the Ages

```
B O O A K J G B L B J E E H V
T L A T X E O N E C M S S F J
B B U J O U L A A N X C S Q L
V O I M R M R L Y H F O A F E
Y O G D E D I A E T C F C J C
G Z A M R N F R Q R A F U B H
N I P E P K T L O E F I D E I
N Z A M C J A H A M N E G I L
K B A U C X I N A B Z R P M D
O Z P M M E R O T L W E N D I
K M W J X O D F A B Z U R J E
B O C U S E A H W D C L Q T V
E V F Q P I R P E Q I I Y E L
E A G L S Z X R J G X W X S U
N O H C U B O R A S U X J T T
```

Say Cheese!

```
A L M P V W P V J G U O L Y N
G L O A D K K A O M S N Q U W
I O L E N O P R A C S A M K X
L T G E G C G B T E C I P J E
V M R A R O H R R H S G E P J
O N I A N A E E I A I C W B
J S T Z V B Z D G V E M O A Z
A R O M M A D Z E O P R R T D
L L K E P A H A O H O A I T L
A B M S R C U J B M K P N O V
I A P R O V O L O N E A O C E
C B R G W Z U K C L H N K I Y
E R E Y U R G V I A E F F R K
B G O U D A S E F X S Z P P K
V N L Y B Q B T D A G E Z P U
```

Bread, Bread, Bread

```
P I T A H D E Z N G R P H C A
N A J K C Z V T I S U I P H T
T A C K J K D J T M M Z P A T
I H A W T C V M P E I E P L A
U R S N J F M E N K U A V L B
C H G U O D R U O S I G C A A
S Q N R Q N B L I C G H A H I
I W X K I I Y R A R A Y S B C
B O K C L P J C I P A A V U X
V M K A Z U C Q A O V B V A M
I E S X L O U T K A C S R O I
L Q P G F H I A L B G H F A I
D L O U T O R T I L L A E G B
S I C X M C Z Z A H T A R A P
E H S C E S L D T I W G L G G
```

In the Kitchen

```
F I B T C I T L K H F S L E D
N R Y G Z A A E I N A O N P H
I O A Q Z D S X L U I A X R J
Q T G Y L I Y S C L L F M O J
C A V E H O S E E P I L E C G
L R W S I U P Q O R R K P E O
W E H F E A P R M E O S S S W
A G P R N T C D D S R L W S I
L I Q S S I K N Y I M J E O G
U R S Y M R E D N A L O C R A
T F P S T L T O A S T E R N R
A E O C B S G S P Y W N E V O
P R O U P D I S H W A S H E R
S G N E G C J E L L Z Y Q H F
B G B G A H H V S D I F K Q H
```

The Baker's Pantry

```
S Y O B E T A L O C O H C X S
O H Z M A K B F X D N A Z H G
O H D X P K L X M V L L O S G
Y Z R C H O I S K L M R A M E
O S J O U C T N I M T K Y S S
S K Y R N L O N G E T N F F E
C H E N A O A C N S A B M I S
I S Z S U V M I O K O K M Y S
B U T T E R N A T A I D X C A
I G X A X G O H N S V H A R L
C V C R G H I O E N A S R E O
Y C D C C V E V J E I E Q A M
A I Z H S U K Z C W W G Y M Z
K C R E R A G U S E X E V S B
V C Q N Y E H B C U R L K R O
```

It's Five O'Clock Somewhere

```
T K B S A P D I U C B S I A B
K E I O A T N P A F X A R S X
B T L L U I I I T K P Z I O D
Y H O M T L P R C L S E U M Y
J M D R I I E N A K T R Q I S
A K A Y R G J V E G B A I M C
C M F I B V U L A G R C A O R
Z R N S I D E C A R R A D A E
I H O T I J O M M Y D O M E W
A D K K K E K F U R F I N E D
C O S M O P O L I T A N E I R
X N A T T A H N A M K R W R I
W W U H J G F S M B R T E T V
F P P S Y U B L T W T Y S N E
J Q E W H B S E S D S N D W R
```

What's Your Pasta?

```
E N N E P U W Q C B T G F E S
E N I D A F L A M O F W U N P
K Y V A I H V I E S R E S I A
L W L L W A N Y T L L T I U G
W G C Z T I I G T L F R L G H
P T Q A L M E N E A E W L N E
U S P A M M T D I O J R I I T
T P T R E P R Q H T Z X P L T
I I W L C A A Q C E A R X A I
D Y L Z P N I N C D Q C O F K
O E N P F S U R E P G P U F N
K S A L B Y N Y R L D M A B F
I P A D A S R F O X L B X V R
T A G L I A T E L L E E E Q T
R I G A T O N I P P D G K H O
```

From the Apple Orchard

```
O G U M P O X F Q D X R P L D
Q E A P V B H H L V E Q I G S
A H M L S A K O M D E I N P Z
U S E A A I G B D W M U K T M
Q O M U C A R E R A H Z L S O
T T F K N Y L C C A V Q A F G
U N S O U I N O Y D E T D R F
S I J N C F U J I E Q B Y G A
T C R I T N L B V V N D U P R
U M O E R I P M E V K O C R Q
M U E H I S X M K B E P H H N
S U E C K S O T R A Z Y M V G
I B D L R R K D T Z X N Z O Z
H H T I M S Y N N A R G W M N
V B M C O R T L A N D U H B S
```

Meet Your Meat

```
P E T S A O R B I R F C T T E
C S S T K T P Q L L D M S E T
D S G U Q N F S A M O R A N E
Y C D C O Q R N O J L R O D K
T N W R X H K W R Z F N R E S
P I R T S K R O Y W E N K R I
G R O U N D B E E F F B C L R
H A N G E R B N T L C D U O B
D R P V L Z I A R Y F H I T
B E I K Z O G T R Y O H C N R
G V G B L I O R T O P F O I
A T C R E R U A Z T R I K S T
Z O I N O Y H C I A O O D E I
D S S N N R E W F H Z N H S P
R F Q A P X K K T Y Z U L S P
```

The Spice Rack

```
C A C H R N D M V C P R R Z J
F I J L U E N R A Q E U E S I
I A R T O B J R C D E A D F M
R U M E S V D M N H K L W E N
S E D N M A E A K I N I O N E
G T V Q M R I S R L V B P N P
A Y A O Y R U P S U L I I E P
L A M R O B A T E S Y R L L K
L W A C A P F I V E S P I C E
S A N X L N I M U C X V H G W
P R T J Q T I X Q Y V F C Q K
I A G U P R E S A F F R O N A
C C Y W H W J B E L H M V B C
E K D D N O M A N N I C Z R Q
A T P T E S O S I R T B Q V F
```

Salad Bar 101

```
L D S C W U E B C J S Y R K
A W S K E C Y H F H J X G E X
U K U N U L I L P E Q Q I B P
S I K T O C E E I E B O P M D
Y N T W K T P R T S A D Z U S
J E A P W P U I Y E C K K C U
L M E E E I L O C C O R B U G
H A B R B I S I R K N T H C F
S O T A M O T S G C B R V X Y
C A R R O T E D X I I X S J T
I P G T R T E N Y N T J N L Y
D R E B D B B K U F S O I I X
K K N U T S D N N B I H V R B
L J E I K J U U J N U A Z L S
T G N G G Z D F O C G V P V S
```

Sushi, Please

```
Y P K Z V Q H I J A G V J F Y
M N S K H H H A S K R S Z H T
B S F V O C Q Q M Y Q A Q I N
V P E T A E H D B A G B W R H
V Z A P M O R O T Q C A V A L
X T N O N A E M T J S H X M S
E A V K E C D W R A V Y I E H
K V Q I C J B E K N A I V F W
I U O B M V P E G R X F H V T
M T T O S P O Z U F Q X X A Z
D L M T T G Y K U N A G I N G
N G R A S E I M E N T A I K O
H W E F G E C Y T W L Y A I Q
D P P Z V J A B S O R U G A M
K Y K O N T L I W C S S L M J
```

Umami Bombs

```
B L O I T D F T N P P O Q B P
Y O V L O L R Y R A U T S N W
T S T H I U J A W R H T H Z B
R U V T F V G Z S M C U L O C
E N A F A E E E B E T I D G T
X C L R N R I S N S E C U M P
V E U I K V G Z U A K S F G R
S T V A O R W A Y N Y O I H J
E R I H S R E T S E C R O W M
A D C V C Y W U T L D P O Y I
E N X M S E O T A M O T R R S
A K I M C H I S S S H T C S O
W R W D U N M Y M J P W V E P
V W B D A Z R P Q J G E L O T
M U S H R O O M S G P L T X A
```

TV Chefs

```
N S I I T N E R U A L E D F B
R A N O M Y S E L A W S O N R
R A M A O L L S E Y T B F Y O
O A M D R L I S I A B I N A W
K P Y S L O K A I N E E G L N
D Q E K A O C G F R T L B F T
F L E N X Y G A I R I Q E D G
B Q N Y T N J L A S B O X C W
S Z M A H K G G O A Y T D Q H
I Y B X C E X T A B M O L R A
Z O S C J P E G N I P K D V Q
F J M S X W O C E U M F L J W
B F I M B W W S Z M X Z I H I
R T V R E W U A G F T S A I C
G P Q W E P R Y K M K U E R K
```

So, How Is It?

```
A G Q N Y N Y C Q E E A Y Z D
C Q H C Q G H H Y E O O G E Y
Z D I X F X C E B B D O L B N
H P Z N T T N E E G C K C Q O
S F S I F S U S N R C C U V M
B P E P P E R Y I I F Y S H E
S I O O N Z C S P Y J L O S L
A B T U X I P S J H H H A V J
L M T T I Y B L A N D G X K W
T T C P E Z A O P H P T U I Y
Y I F A U R O Y X X V J W O K
P R N C X X Q K Y U G G U M D
V V G T B B E N M A V F S T Q
W Q H D G E X D W N F F F R L
Y M A E R C L T L I W W O X L
```

Coffee for All

```
B F O L F K F A R O E A P W R
E T I S N L F X T X T A Z R E
I U S E S F A A F A I L A I V
B F X A O E I T T Q H H N S O
F K M G O H R S T C W Z D T R
U W A I C R I P A E T X L R U
L T D C A R K P S Q A F Z E O
O A A D A R P R C E L S H T P
N M T B L U K U A M F X F T M
A E V T C P I R D D L O C O O
W N J C O N A C I R E M A M C
T U I E R E D E Y E P Y Q L H
P N W M I A N U O S I A L A A
O N I T R O B R E W B F U I G
O N C M Q E R J F V V O B J F
```

Eat Your Veggies

```
R P M Z E I S N F Y C A S D N
L E T T G K E B M E O F P O S
E T W U G U K O R O N F C U Z
E I D O P B O S N O R N G F S
K R B Z L V H K T M C A E P G
S O T F A F C C F O R C I L O
S Y A M N H I O C A R N O J H
Z F K F T F T L P P R R B L D
C E L E R Y R S U U N O A H I
V E G A B B A C T A K G K C X
M U S H R O O M S C C A J A H
J K O S B R E A H F L E T N A
X G O C P P G O W E B L N I E
D J L M D X Y M H B F M X P P
T Z N T O V J I S Z I F U S R
```

Wine Grapes

```
W E R Q G A K W S O T H W V O
D C A U E E J H D E G V F V N
M K J C W S R I M Z I A B C I
G Y M C R G E P X O C J U Q T
Z U R H O N R V G W N J Y M N
H V I E Y A N N O D R A H C E
X P E N N A I W S I M U R M M
V E S I Q E L O Z A G I R O R
U R L N R Y Y B G C O N I E E
T L I B A G B F A N E L A K V
C P N L X V C D T R R B Q S O
L H G A S D N O I M I T L H I
R Z I N F A N D E L O N M A M
E B T C S I S Y R A H J O U M
M L G E P A R E B R A B J B P
```

It's the Rice

```
P Q Q Y S X Q B K T K C T P E
T W O U E S L A A G E O J O U
Q U M T U B T E N D D N Y D L
J A E Q T S W E D S G G I F U
N A X B U O R S E I E E N I I
C L M D Q O S I U Z R E A H V
C T O B G H R I V D E R Y K D
F N A I A I L M R Z E Q R J Q
G A S H G L P A B M I B I B A
C A L I D P A E L L A D B T U
N A N I V I K Y I H S U S S W
N O Z L P Y G L A B E H C I Y
O A M V E Q S G T N M Y Y G I
H M J J O L L O F R I C E C W
I M G I G T N O Q Q W U M V N
```

Ah, the Aroma

```
R A T D L T P E D O X V B M J
L O J O L A V E N D E R L O A
A R S D M W Y O V O F E M M S
Y U T E U A M R R W M B N A M
M Q T Z M A G E D O Y S Z D I
Z I B L N A G R N V O E R R N
L Y N N R A R G E T Y O R A E
L E I T N Z R Y H B E E I C R
B C E O M A S E V O L C Q L V
K R G F S Y L P M T C M R A U
G M A S F I Z C T B N U E C W
Z Z X V S O W F D W S D H X
O Y Y A W F C C U M I N N Q G
B J B I W P E B R H T O I O O
E T A L O C O H C I N Q G V L
```

Time for Breakfast

```
H B A R O K B W L A E M T A O
F A E E Y Y A B P Y U O L W A
V G S M S F R B Q E O W H S B
N E H H F C D A S I T G O F V
B L C L B A O L T P X P R M L
I S E P T R I N C N B A I Q S
E S G O T Y O G E C X N K H N
Y R F L S A V W O S E C K E I
C E R E A L L R N G P A O X F
F R E N C H T O A S T K Z P F
T E L E M O K S N N L E R S U
V W M G F N U J E A O S T G M
I A M N D A Q X U E R C G G W
J Z F E S K K S N A Y G A E D
M S I A W N J W Y V Y P I B F
```

Peppers, Hot and Sweet

```
E C B A B F Y C Y T C P N A O
N N U C N H K N T Q L E P N Q
O Q N B Z A O Y P O R I S B U
H L Y E A D H Z A K Q E A U K
F W L C Y N P E S U R M N V O
G F Q I S A E V I F C J A T N
P N I L J U C L L M F L N R S
A O Q L S A L J L K T E A L N
O R O J H O U B A E M N B H Q
I E R D I P C G J I B E L L G
X N L Y S X W A P O B L A N O
A A T O H O N E P A L A J P S
P B Q X I N O N A R R E S E V
M A H L T O D I U N H V V D U
S H D L O B L Q C D J Q X J A
```

Speaking French

```
O Q L E G T Y B P M E R R K E
J C K S U R A E I L N I N L S
M V P S J Y P R F S L W L C I
F Q A I J M E F T L Q I S R O
P P J A S C U S E E U U B E C
T L C B L O E T N O T A E P I
C C G A S C T R T G O A L E N
A X I L V E F A E S R Y T S S
S R D L S Z T Q D G N G B I K
S C L I W A V E L O U T E Y N
O T V U R C H O U C R O U T E
U X N O N I V U A Q O C G G X
L E K B V E H C I U Q T B T B
E M U G Y A A B B E A W M V R
T H G N Z Q R C V P P X U P Z
```

CROSSWORDS

Biscuits

```
A B O W L ■ T A M E ■ M I L K
L A N A I ■ A M A L ■ A R I A
S H I R K ■ L U L L ■ N O S Y
O A T M E A L R A I S I N ■ ■
■ ■ ■ T N N ■ ■ Y O U A ■ ■ ■
■ ■ C H O C O L A T E C H I P
C I A ■ H O A ■ ■ T S A R S ■
O R C ■ C O O K I E S ■ T I A
R A T I O ■ E S L ■ ■ E S T ■
A N I M A L C R A C K E R ■ ■
■ ■ A T E A ■ ■ I N N ■ ■ ■
■ S N I C K E R D O O D L E ■
O R E O ■ A I D E ■ W R E A K
R I L L ■ R E I D ■ I M A K E
G O L D ■ S R T A ■ S O L E S
```

Bloom

```
A B A G ■ S C A M ■ T A C I T
N A D A ■ W A S I ■ O M A R A
A R I L ■ I R O C ■ L I L A C
I B E A ■ S O U R ■ A G L E T
S Q U A S H B L O S S O M ■ ■
■ ■ P I E ■ ■ L O T ■ E R E
S N A P D R A G O N ■ S N O W
E A G L E ■ P E A ■ A P O S E
T I R E ■ C O R N F L O W E R
A L E ■ H A L ■ A T T ■ ■
■ E D I B L E F L O W E R S
R I M E S ■ O T I C ■ E M I T
I R E N E ■ O H N O ■ L A D E
P A N S Y ■ N A A N ■ D I G A
E S T E E ■ E N L S ■ S L E D
```

Brunch

```
E F F S ■ E M M A ■ T O M E N
B U R L ■ L E A S ■ A L I T O
B R E A K F A S T ■ I D A H O
■ A W N ■ O A R ■ M I N ■ ■
A S K ■ O R A N G E J U I C E
D E S K T O P ■ E X E S ■ ■
A L O E ■ P E P ■ H E E ■ ■
B L U E B E R R Y M U F F I N
■ T P A ■ Y E A ■ U F O S ■
■ O N C E ■ S C A L E N E ■
F R E N C H T O A S T ■ C S C
E E N ■ A C S ■ E A T ■ ■
L A T T E ■ H O M E F R I E S
I D E A S ■ E L A N ■ A V E O
S Y R U P ■ D E E D ■ B E L T
```

College Food

```
B R E W ■ P I Z Z A ■ R I C E
O E N O ■ A C O I N ■ A T A T
B A C K ■ R A N O N ■ M E M O
S C H ■ H E L E N ■ L E M O N
■ H I T O N ■ ■ I O N ■ ■
■ L E F T O V E R S ■ F O E
■ T A N ■ S P I R E ■ P R A Y
J A D E ■ ■ T S A ■ R O T E
A R A T ■ R I O T S ■ O Z S
G A S ■ M I C R O W A V E ■
■ S A M ■ ■ I R O N Y ■
S C E N T ■ A P P L E ■ F I R
P A P A ■ S T E A L ■ P O E T
E R I C ■ A T A L E ■ R O L E
D E C K ■ D A T E D ■ O D D S
```

Italian

```
U T E P █ P A S T A █ L O O P
M A L I █ A R T A S █ I N R E
A R I Z █ A T E I T █ N E B S
M O Z Z A R E L L A █ G R I T
I S A A C █ S E E █ G U S T O
█ █ S E T I █ D A L I █ █
E T A █ I A S █ F U N G H I
C H I C K E N P A R M E S A N
G E L A T O █ A M O █ A M A
█ L E N A █ A S A P █
S A G A L █ S I R █ P I N U P
I T E M █ M I N E S T R O N E
E T T A █ B A S T E █ O R Z O
N A I R █ A G A T E █ G A I N
A R T I █ S O D O M █ I S P S
```

Lunch

```
B A G E L █ B L T █ J E L L Y
A L E R O █ L E O █ U T I L E
R O A R S █ I N S I N C E R E
T U N A S A N D W I C H █
█ █ T E S █ I N T █ S P H
P O T A S S I U M █ U V U L A
E N H █ E N L █ C R A V E N
P E A N U T B U T T E R A N D
P I N U P S █ R A S █ R U M
E D I C T █ L U N C H T I M E
R A N █ O D E █ A I R █
█ C H I C K E N S A L A D
T R I M E S T E R █ S U E D E
R O T O R █ O P S █ E M A I L
I N A N E █ R T E █ D A N T E
```

Quote

```
C H A T █ L I E S █ M O A T S
R O N I █ U N T O █ U M B E R
A N N E █ N A N U █ M O O N S
F O O D W A S A L A B O R █
T R Y █ E R E █ F R A █ I D S
█ █ B Y C O O K I N G I T
S A L E M █ N O S █ L I N O
A W A R D █ T I D █ J E N G A
L A N I █ O H O █ I R E S T
A N D E A T I N G I T
D D R █ S T E █ E T S █ D O A
█ O F L O V E Y O U F E L T
M O V I E █ I P S O █ E V I L
S T E L E █ S E E K █ D I V A
S C R A P █ H E R A █ S L E W
```

Soup

```
P O E M █ I N E P T █ T I E R
R A G E █ S A R A H █ O N Z A
O R G S █ A T I D E █ M A I M
█ C H I L I C O N C A R N E
G S A █ F L O █ F O O T M E N
U P R I S I N G █ R O O █
M A T O █ A R A T E █ E T D
B R O C C O L I C H E D D A R
O E N █ R I S E R █ I S L A
█ A O L █ F O O D S H O P
O O H L A L A █ P B A █ E N E
C H I C K E N N O O D L E █
C A T O █ A N O L I █ E R G O
A R A T █ S E M I S █ E A R N
M A T T █ E X I S T █ K N O T
```

Sweets

S	E	T		A	S	L	A	M		M	A	D	A	M
H	E	H		N	E	E	D	A		A	L	E	R	T
O	L	E		S	L	A	I	N		R	I	S	E	S
R	E	D	V	E	L	V	E	T	C	A	K	E		
T	R	O	I		E	U	R	O		E	R	G	O	
E	S	T	A	D	O	S		A	M	A		T	I	N
		C	O	C	O	A		E	L	M	E	R	S	
	F	R	O	Z	E	N	C	U	S	T	A	R	D	
C	R	I	M	E	A		E	N	T	E	R			
I	O	C		D	N	A		T	O	R	I	N	O	S
A	M	E	N		I	T	S	A		N	A	R	C	
	D	U	T	C	H	A	P	P	L	E	P	I	E	
C	A	I	R	O		E	X	P	O	S		L	O	N
P	A	S	S	E		N	O	E	N	D		E	L	I
A	S	H	E	S		A	N	D	E	S		S	E	C

Zest

O	P	S		S	T	E	P		A	S	M	A	R	A
P	A	P		C	I	A	O		R	H	I	N	O	S
E	P	I		H	O	R	S	E	R	A	D	I	S	H
C	A	C	A	O		E	R	E		I	S	E	E	
	L	E	M	O	N	G	R	A	S	S				
	E	L	S	E			T	A	P	E	R	S		
T	S	A	R		A	N	D	A		L	A	N	A	I
B	A	S	I	L		U	R	L		T	R	Y	S	T
A	L	I	C	E		S	E	A	T		S	A	P	S
R	E	P	A	S	T		R	E	A	L				
	S	E	S	A	M	E	S	E	E	D				
A	W	O	L		L	E	T		E	Y	E	R	S	
V	A	N	I	L	L	A	B	E	A	N		R	I	A
O	N	E	S	I	E		A	R	T	S		I	N	G
N	E	S	T	E	R		T	R	E	E		E	K	E

Consumer Reports

B	O	S	C		A	F	A	R		H	O	W	D	Y
A	R	L	O		S	O	R	E		O	C	H	R	E
S	N	O	W	W	H	I	T	E		S	T	E	E	P
K	E	G		E	E	L		S	P	E	A	R	S	
E	R	A	S	E	S		S	E	E	D	L	E	S	S
T	Y	N	E		F	U	S	S		V	E	T		
		D	O	O	R	S		E	A	T	E	R	Y	
	H	A	R	R	Y	P	O	T	T	E	R			
G	U	I	N	E	A		E	X	A	M	S			
O	P	T		N	A	N	O		L	A	M	B		
A	C	T	O	F	G	O	D		E	N	A	M	O	R
	L	A	C	I	E	R		J	L	O		A	S	A
N	O	B	E	L		T	H	E	G	R	I	N	C	H
I	S	L	A	M		A	U	D	I		O	D	O	M
T	E	E	N	S		S	H	I	N		S	A	W	S

A Visit to the Bakery

S	H	A	R	P		C	H	E	F		D	E	B	S
P	O	W	E	R		M	A	W	R		A	S	A	P
C	H	O	C	O	L	A	T	E	E	C	L	A	I	R
A	O	L		G	A	S		R	E	A	L	I	T	Y
	S	R	I			B	R	A						
B	U	T	T	E	R	C	R	O	I	S	S	A	N	T
A	S	H	E	S		R	U	S	E		S	A	O	
S	E	E	M	S		U	N	C		E	P	C	O	T
I	T	O		L	E	I	A		M	I	A	M	I	
C	O	C	O	N	U	T	C	R	E	A	M	P	I	E
	I	O	S			R	N	A						
M	E	R	L	O	T	S		F	A	A		B	I	B
B	L	A	C	K	F	O	R	E	S	T	C	A	K	E
A	L	G	A		U	N	I	T		E	A	S	E	L
S	E	E	N		L	Y	M	E		S	T	E	A	L

Backyard Barbecue

R	A	I	N	■	M	U	S	S	■	■	T	A	L	C
O	B	O	E	■	O	S	A	K	A	■	A	S	I	A
B	U	T	T	E	R	F	L	Y	S	H	R	I	M	P
E	T	A	■	D	A	L	E	■	S	A	M	S	O	N
■	■	O	I	L	■	■	T	U	N	A	■	■	■	■
S	T	U	F	F	E	D	P	O	R	K	C	H	O	P
C	U	R	L	Y	■	R	O	L	E	S	■	A	N	A
E	L	B	A	■	G	E	N	T	S	■	P	Y	R	E
N	S	A	■	C	R	A	Z	E	■	S	E	E	Y	A
T	A	N	D	O	O	R	I	C	H	I	C	K	E	N
■	■	R	A	C	Y	■	■	O	R	K	■	■	■	■
B	Y	R	O	T	E	■	C	L	U	E	■	T	V	S
T	O	P	S	I	R	L	O	I	N	S	T	E	A	K
E	L	M	S	■	Y	O	K	E	D	■	O	M	N	I
N	O	S	Y	■	■	P	E	N	S	■	O	P	E	N

Small Appliances

A	L	I	A	■	C	U	B	E	■	S	M	E	L	T
M	E	N	U	■	U	N	I	X	■	E	E	R	I	E
P	A	T	T	I	P	A	G	E	■	A	N	N	A	L
■	F	O	O	D	P	R	O	C	E	S	S	O	R	■
■	■	■	C	L	A	M	■	■	V	I	C	■	■	■
E	S	P	R	E	S	S	O	M	A	C	H	I	N	E
A	H	E	A	D	■	■	P	I	N	K	■	N	O	N
S	E	C	T	■	C	E	R	T	S	■	D	E	F	T
E	R	A	■	D	A	T	A	■	■	H	I	R	E	E
S	A	N	D	W	I	C	H	T	O	A	S	T	E	R
■	■	■	E	A	R	■	■	U	C	L	A	■	■	■
■	M	I	C	R	O	W	A	V	E	O	V	E	N	■
S	E	R	I	F	■	H	E	A	L	S	O	V	E	R
A	S	I	D	E	■	A	R	L	O	■	W	I	R	E
T	A	S	E	D	■	T	O	U	T	■	S	L	O	P

Useful Utensils

J	A	W	S	■	B	O	B	A	■	P	H	E	W
A	L	I	T	■	N	O	I	R	S	■	L	A	V	A
V	E	G	E	T	A	B	L	E	P	E	E	L	E	R
A	S	S	E	R	T	■	S	W	E	L	T	E	R	S
■	■	■	L	O	U	D	■	■	N	O	H	■	■	■
M	E	A	S	U	R	I	N	G	S	P	O	O	N	S
O	C	T	■	T	A	P	I	R	■	E	R	R	O	L
D	O	S	E	■	L	O	G	O	S	■	A	B	B	Y
E	L	E	N	A	■	L	E	O	N	A	■	I	L	E
M	E	A	T	T	H	E	R	M	O	M	E	T	E	R
■	■	■	E	R	E	■	■	S	C	U	D	■	■	■
I	R	A	N	I	A	N	S	■	A	S	I	A	G	O
M	O	R	T	A	R	A	N	D	P	E	S	T	L	E
P	L	I	E	■	T	R	I	O	S	■	O	M	A	N
S	E	E	S	■	H	Y	P	E	■	■	N	E	M	O

Vegetable Garden

T	I	P	S	■	A	D	M	I	T	■	M	E	L	B
A	D	A	M	■	R	O	O	N	E	■	A	L	O	U
J	A	L	A	P	E	N	O	P	E	P	P	E	R	S
■	■	A	R	I	A	■	■	U	N	I	■	N	E	C
B	U	T	T	E	R	N	U	T	S	Q	U	A	S	H
I	R	A	■	R	U	I	N	■	Y	U	M	■	■	■
D	A	B	S	■	G	E	L	S	■	E	A	R	P	■
E	L	L	E	■	S	C	O	O	P	■	S	E	L	A
■	S	E	A	M	■	E	C	R	U	■	S	E	E	D
■	■	■	R	I	M	■	K	E	P	T	■	D	A	D
B	R	U	S	S	E	L	S	S	P	R	O	U	T	S
E	E	L	■	O	N	E	■	■	E	E	O	C	■	■
B	E	E	F	S	T	E	A	K	T	O	M	A	T	O
O	V	E	R	■	O	C	H	E	R	■	P	T	A	S
P	E	S	O	■	S	H	I	N	Y	■	H	E	R	E

Chefs and Their Books

```
T O R A H . I T E M . S T A T
E L I S E . D O R A . M E R E
R A C H A E L R A Y . A X E D
N Y E . D Y E S . G R A N D
. G O R D O N R A M S A Y
I P H O N E . O A T .
M I T T . M A N G O . F D A
A N T H O N Y B O U R D A I N
N A P . M A M A S . O V E N
. E P A . P I R A T E
W O L F G A N G P U C K .
O P E R A . F A M E . D E E
N I N A . J U L I A C H I L D
K N I T . O M A N . A I S L E
Y E N S . E A T S . P E C A N
```

Edible Movies

```
S A P P Y . A C E D . S I B S
A T R I A . G A M E . T O R I
C H I C K E N R U N . O N E G
H E N S . L E E . A L I E N
E A T . M Y S T I C P I Z Z A
T R E V I . M A P . E E L
. T R O L L . B A S . A D D S
. L A Y E R C A K E .
J A P E . R D A . S N O G S
E A R . F I N . E N O K I
A M E R I C A N P I E . T I M
L I C I T . E S P . S O A P
O L E G . N A C H O L I B R E
U N D O . O R C A . A R E E L
S E E R . M E O W . M I D A S
```

Farmers' Market

```
A R C S . I D A H O . O P T S
H E A P . F A D E R . N E W T
A P P L E S T O R E . O N E A
. L I A R . A R M . O F T E N
J E T T A . P E A C H F U Z Z
E T A . S A L . N A Y . P E A
B E L L . M A P . P O M .
. B A N A N A S L U G S .
. W I Z . R U E . M O N A
A T L . C O Q . N T H . C O X
G R A P E N U T S . A G A T E
H I K E R . O O H . M O L E
A V E R . F R U I T S A L A D
S I R S . B U T N O . P E S O
T A S E . I M S E T . E D Y S
```

Catch of the Day

```
D E L I . M A Y D A Y . T B S
I V A N . A M O E B A . H A L
N I C H O L A S R A Y . E Y E
O C T A V E . H E S . C H O P
S T O L E . M I K E T R O U T
. F R E E . S A A B .
P D F . A M O S . U M B E R
C H R I S T O P H E R P I K E
S L O M O . S T E W . T E N
. M A M A . D E A R .
L A N C E B A S S . H E F T Y
E R O S . O D E . I A G R E E
V O W . J U L I A N B R E A M
E M O . A N A K I N . E S S E
R A N . I D I O M S . T H E N
```

Fruit Basket

```
ALVA  PERES  AJAR
REIN  EXALT  COVE
FIONAAPPLE  THEN
 LARGO  END  ANT
WHALER  MRORANGE
EATS  AWAY  OWNER
BRO  OVER  COO
 PROFESSORPLUM
 NFL  DIAS  NOW
FLOES  MELB  LINE
LIZLEMON  CRAVAT
AVA  TAT  SAUCE
MERE  CHUCKBERRY
ELKS  EENIE  USER
SYST  DRESS  PENS
```

Get to the Popcorn

```
USPS  ESSA  CSPAN
POLE  VIAL  OTOWN
SLOT  ATNO  GEESE
HAUTECUISINE
ARGON  SCALPEL
WAH  TWAS  SCHEME
 ARETHA  EDIE
 BABETTESFEAST
RAGU  ABSURD
OMEGAS  ANNE  INC
CASSIUS  COCOA
 LOVESKITCHEN
ANVIL  ROUT  TIVO
SCIFI  TIDE  ERIE
HOMES  ATOM  TOLD
```

Listen

```
LAPS  CIRCA  OWNS
IBET  OCEAN  POET
MERE  MEANT  ARTY
BLUEBERRYHILL
 LOT  ORG  DEA
LCD  GREENONIONS
AHOT  URL  IDRIS
BROS  EATIT  EDGE
RONAN  OSH  SEMS
AMERICANPIE  RAS
TES  NHL  RRS
 BREADANDROSES
CLUE  NOMAD  FATE
PERF  CUPPA  TINE
AMYS  ESSAY  CLAP
```

Off the Rack

```
RAHM  NIL  JAPAN
ALIAS  EKE  USAGE
CURRYTOEXTREMES
IMEASY  HOA
SNO  RANFOR  WAS
MINTFORYOU  PICK
 TOLDTO  FIFTY
SAXON  MIT  RAISE
TEMPT  OMAHAN
ARES  OREGANOSIN
RON  PRESET  TCU
 EAT  ESPIER
THYMEONHERHANDS
NORMA  AUG  ARGUE
SUSAN  PEG  TSPS
```

The Chef

C	A	S	A	S		S	F	P	D		O	N	M	E
O	T	E	R	I		P	A	R	E		N	E	A	R
S	T	E	E	L		A	Z	O	V		R	O	D	E
M	U	S	S	E	L	M	E	M	O	R	Y			
I	N	T	O	N	E				T	H	E	D	O	T
C	E	O		T	V	S		G	E	E		I	P	O
		S	K	I	P	P	E	D	A	B	E	E	T	
A	B	R	A		O	A	T			U	T	N	E	
G	R	A	P	E	S	O	C	I	E	T	Y			
T	I	P		M	T	N		N	T	H		O	V	A
S	E	S	A	M	E			T	I	E	R	E	D	
		N	A	A	N	S	T	A	N	D	A	R	D	
S	T	U	N		L	O	O	K		A	U	T	O	S
M	A	K	I		T	A	F	T		I	C	O	N	O
S	U	R	E		H	A	T	S		R	E	R	A	N

KATE HEDDINGS was the food editor at *Food & Wine* magazine for more than seventeen years. She is the coauthor of *The Good Book of Southern Baking: A Revival of Biscuits, Cakes, and Cornbread* with chef Kelly Fields. She is currently a contributing editor at *Food & Wine* and has written for the *Washington Post* and Thrillist. Find her on Twitter and Instagram at: @katehedd.

CROSSWORD AUTHORS

Puzzles 1-10: Kristy McGowan
Puzzle 11: Jeremy Horwitz
Puzzles 12-16: David Shukan
Puzzles 17-19: Kevin Christian
Puzzles 20-21: David Kwong
Puzzles 22-25: Roy Leban

Bloomfield Township Public
Library

1099 Lone Pine Road
Bloomfield Township, Michigan 48302
(248) 642-5800 | www.btpl.org

31160041140661

THE RECIPES IN THIS BOOK ARE ALL WRONG!

Yes, you read that correctly. Who doesn't love a good puzzle? And what sounds more satisfying than being able to eat your results afterward? If you've ever tried cooking, you will be all too familiar with how puzzling certain recipes can be—from figuring out proper techniques to deciphering confusing instructions. So why not make a game out of it?

In *Hungry Games*, former food editor Kate Heddings embarks on a journey to turn her recipe challenges into a game of recipe repairs, testing the skills of cooks who know it all by intentionally adding errors to each recipe. Ranging from easy to difficult, these recipes contain both cooking mistakes (time, temperature, quantities) and editorial mistakes (out-of-order ingredients, typos, etc.) and bring some fun back to cooking. Also including traditional food-themed word searches and crossword puzzles, *Hungry Games* is perfect for every avid cook or puzzle fan—and gives the phrase "playing with your food" new meaning.

KATE HEDDINGS was the food editor at *Food & Wine* magazine for more than seventeen years. She is the coauthor of *The Good Book of Southern Baking: A Revival of Biscuits, Cakes, and Cornbread* with chef Kelly Fields. She is currently a contributing editor at *Food & Wine* and has written for the *Washington Post* and Thrillist. Find her on Twitter and Instagram at: @katehedd.

GAMES & ACTIVITIES   1020

ISBN 978-1-9821-3613-0   **$14.99 U.S.**/$19.99 Can.

Tiller Press
SimonandSchuster.com
 @simonandschuster
COVER DESIGN BY PATRICK SULLIVAN
MUG BY SERGIOZA24 / SHUTTERSTOCK
PLATE AND SILVERWARE BY RHENZY / SHUTTERSTOCK

PRINTED IN THE U.S.A.